WHO KILLED KENNEDY? was begun in December 1963 and completed after *l'Express*, France's most influential weekly and one of the outstanding liberal publications in the world, assigned Mr. Buchanan to go to Dallas to cover the trial of Jack Ruby. *L'Express* subsequently published a series of Buchanan articles, and these were reprinted in almost every country of the world. In book form, WHO KILLED KENNEDY? has been a tremendous best seller in every country in which it has appeared. The American edition contains many additions and revisions based on material that has come to light since the first appearance of the book—including detailed commentary on the findings of the Warren Commission.

WHO KILLED KENNEDY?

Book XVI

This edition

is especially printed

for the friends of

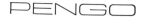

PENGO

EARTH BORING AUGERS • EARTH DIGGING TEETH

TENSION STRINGING EQUIPMENT

IN USE ON EVERY CONTINENT
AROUND THE WORLD

PENGO'S new home in Sunnyvale, California

GERALD A. M. PETERSEN
President

Petersen Engineering Co., Inc.
Pengo Manufacturing Co., Inc.

In the summer and fall of 1964 Mrs. Petersen and I toured Europe and the Near East during which time I worked in 18 different countries. Talk of the brutal assassination of President Kennedy was still an active subject for discussion both in the United States and Europe. Almost every American sincerely believed that Oswald alone killed President Kennedy (even though there was evidence of bullets from opposite directions), however, this seemed completely illogical to the rest of the world. Therefore, I decided to make it a special point to ask those with whom I spoke their opinion of, "who assassinated President Kennedy." I discussed this subject with approximately 130 individuals—waiters, customers, friends, taxi drivers and strangers in the Near East and both East and West Europe. With one lone exception, every one of the 130 were convinced that President Kennedy's assassination had been planned, directed and executed by a powerful organization and that one man could not have done it unaided.

The European reaction was to immediately look for a motive. "Who stands to gain?", they asked. They believe that events will eventually point a finger! Could it be, that the newspaper stories published in the United States on this horrible deed were inaccurate!

During my readings, I came upon Mr. Buchanan's exciting, well-reasoned and thoroughly referenced book "WHO KILLED KENNEDY?" It seemed appropriate to reproduce this significant volume for the permanent libraries of our friends throughout the world. The book, "WHO KILLED KENNEDY?", in my opinion, will remain a lasting, important historical document for as long as the twentieth century remains of interest to all humanity.

Gerald A M Petersen

PRESIDENT

P.S. Please send us your zip code number! A zip code number will be required on all future mailings.

3

PENGO AUGERS

96″ PENGO Auger, largest in new AA super strong series for most powerful drilling machines

36″ PENGO Heavy Duty Auger

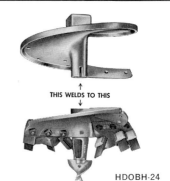

THIS WELDS TO THIS

HDOBH-24

(upper) New, larger 20-A-70 PENGO Wisdom Tooth for AA series augers

(lower) Famous 16-A-50 PENGO Wisdom Tooth

PENGO Flight Auger with Gravel Guards

PENGO Foundation Augers
drill holes to any diameter

16" PENGO Light Duty
Head for use on light
duty diggers—farm
tractor post hole borers,
elevator contractor
borers, etc.

PENGO
Light Duty
Shanks

PENGO
Screw Bit
for small
diameter
holes

PENGO 2" Auger
with Tungsten
Carbide Drill
Head

PENGO Tungsten
Carbide Drill Heads
for drilling rock and
hard abrasive materials

PENGO TEETH are available for Shovels, Hoes, Draglines, Clamshells, Scarifiers and Loaders, etc.

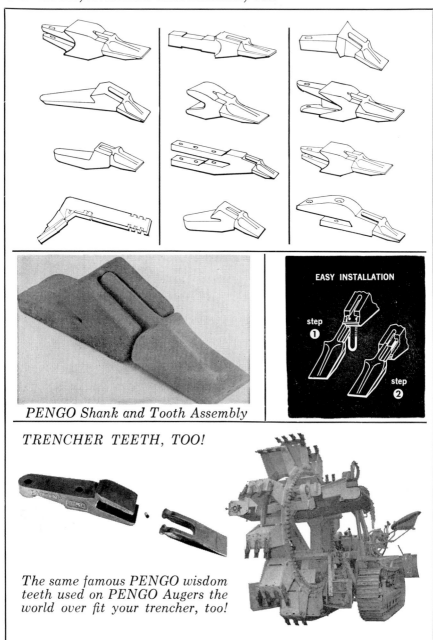

PENGO Shank and Tooth Assembly

EASY INSTALLATION

step ❶

step ❷

TRENCHER TEETH, TOO!

The same famous PENGO wisdom teeth used on PENGO Augers the world over fit your trencher, too!

PENGO Tension-Stringing Equipment

— safest, most economical way to string transmission and distribution lines!

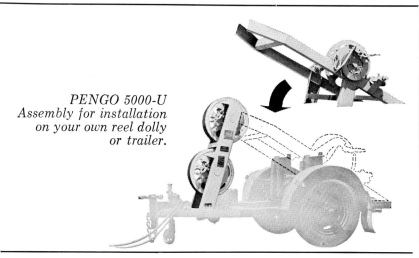

*PENGO 5000-U
Assembly for installation
on your own reel dolly
or trailer.*

*PENGO Model 4000 PM
Pole Mount Tensioner
Takes conductor to .750"
diameter, tensions to
1,000 lbs., can be carried
in every line truck!*

*PENGO Model
5500 BWCP-TR-I
Cable Puller.
Ideal for distribution
line stringing!*

Three PENGO 7000 TR-1-72 tensioners on American Gas & Electric Company's EHV line in Indiana.

Three PENGO 6000 TR-1 tensioners on Idaho Power Company's 230 KV transmission line from Hell's Canyon.

PENGO 5000 STRI economical tensioner for distribution work.

PENGO holds many patents in the U.S.A., Canada, England, Australia and many other countries throughout the world, with other patents pending.

PENGO 7000
TR-I-54
Tensioner

PENGO 6100
TCRW-46
Reel Winder.

PENGO 6700
BWCP TR-I Bull-
wheel Cable Puller
and 6100 TCRW-54
Reel Winder on an
EHV job in the
high mountains of
Arizona.

PENGO Model 6100 HLRC Reel Carrier, rear view. Reel spindle brake is standard equipment. Removable rear tow bar (optional at extra cost) permits towing two or more reel carriers behind truck or tractor.

PENGO Combination Puller-Tensioners — Series 600

PENGO Special Equipment and Accessories

Belling Tools for Tower Footings

PENGO-Miller Swivels

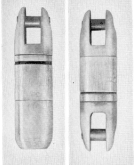
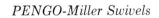

A	B	C
Threaded Cap	*Standard*	*Swedge Cap*

PENGO Pulling Eye

*PENGO Spreader Bars
for setting
H-frame structures.*

Who Killed Kennedy?

THOMAS G. BUCHANAN

G. P. Putnam's Sons New York

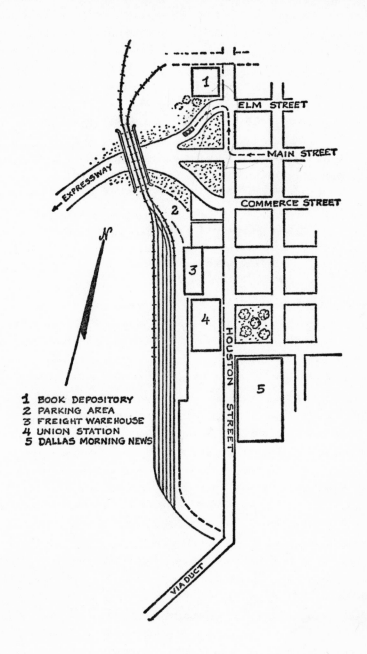

ELM STREET

MAIN STREET

COMMERCE STREET

EXPRESSWAY

HOUSTON STREET

VIA DUCT

N

1 BOOK DEPOSITORY
2 PARKING AREA
3 FREIGHT WAREHOUSE
4 UNION STATION
5 DALLAS MORNING NEWS

Except the Lord keep the city, the watchman waketh but in vain

—the words which John Fitzgerald Kennedy was to have spoken in a city where the watchmen slumbered
—words found in the 127th Psalm of which the next verse follows:

> *It is vain for you to rise up early,*
> *to sit up late,*
> *to eat the bread of sorrows;*
> *For so he giveth his beloved sleep. . . .*

AUTHOR'S NOTE

THE major part of the report you are about to read—extracts of which first appeared in *l'Express* of Paris—was filed in Washington in March, 1964, with the President's Commission on the Assassination of President Kennedy, headed by Chief Justice Earl Warren. This action was taken at the request of a staff member of that commission, Howard P. Willens.

Discussion of the case with a Commission representative followed an interview of more than an hour with Nicholas De B. Katzenbach, at that time Deputy Attorney General of the United States, to whom Attorney General Robert F. Kennedy had delegated most of his responsibilities during the months that followed the assassination. This interview was arranged by Senator Edward M. Kennedy of Massachusetts, the President's younger brother. The subsequent appointment with a representative of the President's Commission was made by Mr. Katzenbach.

ASSASSINATION....

Whether it takes place in Dallas or Petit-Clamart may, in the end, depend upon the momentary trembling of a hand, an instant's indecision....

Fate? Perhaps. But fate is governed by a certain logic.

To explain why, in that fateful moment, one hand trembled and the other hand was calm requires more than a knowledge of psychology. It takes historical perspective. For in no respect do nations differ more completely from each other than in what provokes them to destroy their leaders.

The observer from a Western land in Tokyo during the 1930's could hardly have comprehended how a secret terrorist association, the Black Dragons, could have managed to transfer the government from its opponents to the army, not by one but by a gradual succession of assassinations.

The American, during the days when Algiers, and eventually Paris, grew accustomed to a daily quota of attempted murders with the plastic bomb, felt certain that assassinations perpetrated with the aid of elements of the police and army were peculiarly European.

And the Frenchman, reading any of his magazines or daily papers, is assured the crime of Dallas "could have happened only in a place like Texas."

Both the French and the Americans are right—and both are wrong. For each volcano has its own eruption, and the lava flows according to the nature of the crater.

It will be the function of this book to look down into

9

that crater with the eyes of an American whose ancestors lived in a Southern city where the chief of police, encouraged by some of the most respected citizens, and with the aid of petty criminals recruited from the local bars, set out to kill the President of the United States.

They thought he was a traitor. They believed he was an obstacle to the successful prosecution of a war which they regretted, which they felt their enemies had thrust upon them, but which they regarded as inevitable.

They did not succeed in killing Lincoln. That would come a long time later, at a time when it would serve no purpose but revenge, after a war which Lincoln had resisted to the end—a four-year war that cost America more lives than all the wars America has fought since then. It killed 600,000 people. That is one percent of the anticipated casualties in the United States during the first four hours of a new world war. . . .

*　　　*　　　*

The first reaction of the people of America, on hearing of their President's assassination, was astonishment, and this emotion of surprise was generally shared throughout the world.

"I can't believe it," people kept repeating as they gathered on the streets, around a radio or television set, or telephoned their neighbors. "Is it really true? I don't see how it could have happened."

It was unexpected, in a way that the attack which took place at Petit-Clamart was not. For there already had been one plot to blow up the car the President of France intended to employ for a brief visit to his country home in 1961. Reports were published of at least six other, similar attempts presumed to have been organized by members of the very army that De Gaulle once led. The General was living in an atmosphere of violence and it was not with any feeling of complete amazement that the public learned on August 22, 1962, that General De Gaulle had been attacked by volleys of machine-gun fire and that twelve bullets actually pierced his car and one had missed his head by inches.

Threats to Europe's leaders had been common, in the weeks before the Kennedy assassination. Scotland Yard had been compelled to furnish guards for Harold Wilson, Britain's Labour Party leader, and to post police around his home in order to protect him after threats that he was scheduled to be killed. In Brussels Belgium's King Baudouin received a death threat, and in Stockholm Swedish Premier Tage Erlander had been similarly menaced; while in Bonn the guards were doubled at the home of the West German Chancellor, Ludwig Erhard, after a phone call warned that he would die unless he met war veterans' demands for higher pensions. An Italian threw a fire bomb at the house where the new Pope was born.*

But not in the United States—or so Americans were fond of thinking. On November 22, 1963, when Kennedy was shot, America and the whole world were stunned.

After this first, bewildered disbelief, the impulse of observers everywhere was to assume a link between the Kennedy assassination and the recent violence of Southerners against the Negro. It was felt the forces which, a hundred years before, had been responsible for the attack upon the President who freed the slaves had struck down his successor, who had tried to give dimension to their freedom.

For, indeed, there had been violence in the United States during the months before the President was murdered. There had been a great deal of it, and it had originated and

* The summary of threats to Europe's leaders is based on reports in *U.S. News & World Report*, December 23, 1963.

was being carried out almost exclusively at that time by the advocates of racial segregation. It had taken place in Southern cities just like Dallas. Medgar Evers, the field secretary for the state of Mississippi of the N.A.A.C.P. (National Association for the Advancement of Colored People), largest and traditionally most important Negro organization, was shot in the back and killed after repeated warnings to him to cease all activity for integration of the Negro. White men were no more exempt from murder than the Negroes, if they advocated the enforcement of the Constitution. A white postman, William Moore, who chose to spend his own vacation walking through the South bearing a sign that urged equality for Negroes, was shot down and his dead body left upon the roadside. Finally, in the most shocking crime of all, a bomb was placed inside a Negro church in Birmingham where Negro children gathered for their Bible study, and exploded fatally among them, killing four small girls and wounding others. Yet the murderers in many of these cases were permitted to remain unpunished.

Consequently, even so conservative a leader as Theodore McKeldin, Mayor of Baltimore, the largest and most northern of the Southern cities, had this first reaction to reporters when he heard the President had died: "This is the worst calamity that has befallen the South since the assassination of Lincoln. In both cases a man named Johnson succeeded to the Presidency—Andrew Johnson in the case of Lincoln, and now Lyndon Johnson, which adds to the bitter cup of the South. Police will certainly pick up the assassin, but that is no sign that they will get the real murderers—the men who have been stirring up the malignant hatred that has finally built up into this final explosion."

As McKeldin had expected, the police of Dallas did arrest the man alleged to have committed the assassination and, within the first few hours, although there had been no witnesses and no confession, Dallas law-enforcement officers had reconstructed Lee H. Oswald's crime and said they knew his motive. The assassin, they declared, was a fanatical pro-Communist recently returned from the U.S.S.R., who hated the United States.

Already stunned by the first shock of hearing that the President was dead, the world accordingly received a second blow whose import was, in some respects, still more alarming. It was bad enough that a key figure for the preservation of world peace had been eliminated, when he was so desperately needed. But it had been universally attributed to Southern white-supremacy fanatics and was thus no more than a domestic issue. Suddenly, world peace itself was jeopardized. For if a Communist, allegedly a Moscow-trained assassin, was responsible, then all the progress made toward rapprochement of the East and West within the past twelve months was lost, and the whole world was back where it had been on that October morning when two fleets were sailing toward each other on collision course off the coast of Cuba. If the only suspect, Oswald, was a Communist, then we were certainly not far from that last thermonuclear explosion which both Kennedy and Khrushchev had avoided.

Two groups instantly declared that they did not believe the explanation of the crime which was released in Dallas. One of these was the U.S.S.R. itself, and Communists of other nations siding with the Russians in their controversy with Mao Tse-tung. The Soviet Premier, Nikita S. Khrushchev, who had learned of the attack on Kennedy while he was in Kiev, rushed back at once to Moscow and expressed his personal condolences to the United States Ambassador in Moscow. He described the murder as "a heavy blow to all people who hold dear the cause of peace and Soviet-American cooperation." An announcement of the U. S. Communists condemned the crime and said that Os-

13

wald had not ever been affiliated with their party; and Fair Play for Cuba, of which the police said Oswald was the local chairman, said that if he had requested them to send him leaflets they had doubtless done so, but he was not and had never been a spokesman or official for them, either on a national or local level. Such denials of responsibility were, to a large extent, discounted on the ground that if the Left, indeed, were guilty they would doubtless try to hide it.

But the other group that never placed its faith in the official thesis was the Negro population of the U.S.A. which, from the first few hours, has been close to unanimity in the conviction that the violent white-hooded men with hooded minds who, for a century, have hunted down the Negro in an orgy of castrations and unpunished murders, with their tar and feathers, with their ropes, their rifles, had this time struck down the President of the United States himself because he was considered to have been what, in their rage, right-wing fanatics called a "nigger lover." Thus, for instance, in a headline spread across the top half of the *California Eagle,* the Negro journal flatly stated, NEGROES DOUBT OFFICIAL STORY OF ASSASSINATION. BELIEVE MURDER LINKED TO CIVIL RIGHTS. And Mrs. Juanita Jackson Mitchell, a Southern N.A.A.C.P. official, blamed the slaying on "hatred that has infested the South like a disease. The deaths of Medgar Evers and of the four little girls in Birmingham foreshadowed this day."

There is reason to suppose that a majority of right-wing sympathizers had themselves, at first, assumed that the assassin came from their ranks. Some of them had openly rejoiced at the elimination of a President they hated—as, for instance, in the speech of Richard Ely, president of the Memphis Citizens Council, in which he told the Nashville, Tennessee, White Citizens Council, "Kennedy died a tyrant's death. . . . He encouraged integration, which has the support of communism. He was a tyrant." Other right-wing spokesmen had reacted with a temporary, but no doubt sincere, remorse, like that of James Dobbs, commentator for the "Life Line" right-wing propaganda broadcasts sponsored by the Dallas multimillionaire H. L. Hunt. Robert G. Sherrill of the Miami *Herald,* in an article for the *Nation* February 24, 1964, says Dobbs "burst into tears and said he would have nothing to do with murder." But as soon as it was learned that an alleged pro-Communist had been arrested, the extreme right-wing groups broke their first, embarrassed silence. Armed with the official thesis that the crime had been committed by a man who had not only lived in Russia but was now a Castro propagandist, these groups took advantage of the opportunity to press for execution of a project they had always advocated: to retaliate by an immediate invasion of Cuba. Such an operation, though to Europeans it may seem fantastic, actually was accorded serious consideration by some members of the Congress.

The official charges against Oswald were, in a surprisingly short time, extremely detailed. Never in the history of crime has such an intricate, premeditated murder been so swiftly settled—an accomplishment made even more remarkable by two facts: first, that Oswald said that he had no connection with the crime; and second, no one else had seen him do it who was able to identify him.

Oswald had denied his guilt, but he did not deny his Communist affiliations and, since technically the police appeared to have an "airtight" case against him, nothing now remained except to analyze his motive.

Oswald was, it seemed, an ex-Marine who, having asked for his release from military duty, had a short time later gone to the U.S.S.R., denounced his country and requested citizenship in the Soviet Union. He had lived there and was married to a Russian woman, but after two years informed Senator Tower of Texas that he wanted to come home. He said that he was disillusioned with the Communists, but the police asserted that on his arrival in the U.S.A. he had become involved in new pro-Communist activities. He was, by his own statement, chairman of a local chapter of Fair Play for Cuba, the pro-Castro group in the United States, and he had been arrested in a riot which resulted from the distribution of their leaflets. Many books, said to have been pro-Marxist and pro-Russian, were discovered in his home. Still more incriminating was a photograph reported to have been discovered which showed Oswald with the murder weapon and a copy of *The Worker*,* the official weekly Communist newspaper published in New York.

Clearly, then, it was the thesis of the Dallas law-enforcement agencies that Oswald had committed a premeditated murder to advance the Communist world revolution. He was said to be a Soviet-trained expert at political assassination, who intended to escape to Cuba or to Russia.

If the suspect in this case had lived, the prosecutor would have had to prove "beyond a reasonable doubt" that a Russian-trained, pro-Castro and pro-Communist assassin felt the death of Kennedy would benefit the Soviet Union and the Cuban revolution.

Could a prosecutor prove it?

Nowhere but in the United States could such a charge be made without provoking general derision. The most anti-Communist of Europeans realize the death of Kennedy was more sincerely mourned in Moscow than in any other foreign capital, if only for the fact that leaders of the Soviet Union staked their whole political careers upon the chance of a *détente* with the United States. The Russians had, in their debate with the Chinese, maintained there were two factions in the West: enlightened capitalist leaders, who appreciated that in an atomic war there were no victors,

* Other reports said that the paper was *The Militant,* a Trotskyist publication hostile to *The Worker*.

and the anti-Communist fanatics who believed the nation that struck first could win the war. The chance of peace depended, therefore, on continuance of Khrushchev-Kennedy negotiations, which began so fruitfully with the agreement to curtail the testing of atomic weapons. Khrushchev had withdrawn in anger from the conference in Paris after the U-2 plane incident, proclaiming that there was no use in trying to negotiate with Eisenhower, since his word could not be trusted. He would wait, he said, for the election of the President's successor. After the last Cuban crisis, each of the two leaders, knowing the enormous burden of responsibility the other carried, knowing also that if either had desired a war the conflict could not then have been avoided, grudgingly respected one another and thereafter carefully refrained from any action that would strengthen the domestic opposition of a trusted adversary. Any plot by leaders of the Kremlin to dispatch a trained assassin to shoot down the only President since Roosevelt they respected, and expose the delicate negotiations which were just beginning to the veto of a man whose background bears a certain ominous resemblance, in their eyes, to that of Harry Truman, is no less fantastic than to think that the American Central Intelligence Agency would scheme to murder Khrushchev and replace him with another Stalin.

Neither did the Cubans have the slightest reason to want Lyndon Johnson or Barry Goldwater in the White House. Only three days earlier, in a November 19th interview with the distinguished French journalist Jean Daniel, who was at that time representing *l'Express* of Paris, Fidel Castro had, in fact, declared that although he considered Kennedy could not escape a major portion of the guilt for ordering the Bay of Pigs invasion, "I believe that in the last few months he has come to a better understanding of the situation and, in any case, I am convinced that anyone who might replace him would be worse." Daniel attributes to

17

the Cuban leader the assertion that if peace in North and South America were to be won, "there must arise in the United States a man with the capacity to understand and to adapt himself to the explosive reality of Latin America." For Castro, "this man might, even now, be Kennedy. He still has the full opportunity of becoming, in the eyes of history, the greatest President of the United States—the one who would at last come to a recognition of the fact that there can be a coexistence between capitalists and socialists, even in the American hemisphere. He would then be an even greater President than Lincoln. I know that Khrushchev, for example, considers Kennedy a man with whom it is possible to have discussions. . . . Other people tell me that, before discussions can take place, it will be necessary to await his second term. . . . If you see him again, you can tell him that, if it helps him to win his re-election, I am ready to announce that Goldwater is a friend of mine!" Daniel, in fact, already had a rendezvous with Kennedy which was to have occurred a short time after his return from Dallas. The French reporter had first interviewed the President of the United States on October 24th; he had then gone directly to Havana, where he had a series of discussions with the Cuban leader; he had promised to go back to Kennedy and to deliver Castro's confidential message before either interview was published. It was, in short, an effort through nondiplomatic channels to explore the possibility of normalizing U. S.-Cuban relations. An affirmative response by Kennedy to Castro's trial balloon would have prepared the way for an eventual top-level meeting with the U. S. President—a meeting much less likely to be held with his successor—one which might have stabilized the Castro Government, enabling it to channel funds and labor wasted now on national defense to economic projects desperately needed by the Cuban people. It was not the moment Cuba would have chosen to kill Kennedy. If such an act had been considered, it would have occurred during the period when the United States was sponsoring the Bay of Pigs invasion, or in 1962, when the whole world seemed on the brink of war and Cuba faced direct U. S. invasion.

A more plausible hypothesis, although devoid of any evidence which would support it, is that Kennedy's assassin may have been an agent of the Chinese Communists. This has the merit of at least appearing to have some ideological foundation. From the Chinese point of view, unlike the Russian, Kennedy's assassination was not an event to be regretted. It was, on the contrary, applauded—a reaction which was as absurd as it was shocking. But this demonstration cannot be interpreted as indicating an expected benefit from the assassination, or specific hatred of the individual who had been murdered. It reflected a hostility to *all* Americans—hostility which, after all, is not incomprehensible, considering that Truman had in 1950 sent U. S. troops 5,000 miles across the ocean to the Chinese border to conduct a war which cost more than a million Chinese dead and wounded. If the Chinese did not try to murder Truman, it is hard to understand what motive they could possibly have had for an attack on Kennedy. U. S.-Chinese relations had not undergone substantial change during the Kennedy Administration, but such minor alterations as occurred were, on the whole, improvements. U. S. intervention in Viet Nam continued, but the policy had been established under the preceding, Eisenhower government and it was intensified, after the death of Kennedy, by his successor. Kennedy's opponent in the last election, Nixon, had been an associate of Knowland, the Republican from Nixon's state of California who was known as "Chiang Kai-shek's ambassador" and had led efforts in the U. S. Senate to send weapons to the Nationalist armies for eventual invasion of the Chinese mainland. Kennedy had, on the other hand, declared that if Pekin sent troops to capture Quemoy and Matsu, he did not think these islands off the coast of China could or ought to be defended by the U. S. naval forces. It seems clear that from the Chinese point of view, as from the Soviet and Cuban, no political advantage could have been anticipated from the death of Kennedy.

Nor could a native Marxist have expected any benefit from Kennedy's assassination. Communists had first been prosecuted under Truman, and the policy continued under Eisenhower. By the time the Kennedy Administration took office, membership in the U. S. Communist Party had been reduced from a peak strength of about 100,000 to less than 10,000. There had been no noticeable relaxation under Kennedy in this campaign against domestic Communists, but neither had the effort been intensified. A spokesman for the U. S. Communists had recently announced their membership, after a long decline, was finally beginning to make gains. This tendency might have continued and, indeed, expanded as official anti-Soviet hostility diminished. The first group to suffer, if such tensions were renewed, would be the U. S. Communists themselves. And if it could be shown that U. S. Communists had engineered the crime, the worst excesses which the country knew after the murder of McKinley or during the dominance of Senator McCarthy would have seemed an era of tranquillity and tolerance by contrast with the persecution to which Communists would then have been subjected. It is consequently inconceivable that if the Communists did have this suicidal notion, the assassin would have posed before the crime to have a snapshot taken of himself holding the murder weapon, with a copy of *The Worker,* the official party paper. No conceivable political objective of the U. S. Communists, moreover, has been served by Kennedy's elimination. There appears to have been disagreement in the U. S. party, back in 1960, whether to support the Kennedy campaign or to remain completely neutral. Kennedy had run with Communist support, however. And by 1963, on the main issues of the day—the Negro civil rights drive and disarmament—the President was felt to be an ally—temporary, to be sure, but of a key and, it was later feared, an irreplaceable importance. One has but to read the very issue of *The Worker* Oswald is alleged to have been reading to observe that Kennedy was being treated, at that time, with a respect not far removed from admiration. To the Communists of the United States, the President's domestic foes were their foes, also. And Gus Hall, a national official, had asserted that the party should endorse the President for re-election in the 1964 campaign. One scarcely sees why any Communist would murder the man they considered as the most progressive candidate who had a reasonable chance to be elected.

The assassination of the President may thus be shown to have served no political objective which can reasonably be attributed to the domestic Communists or, for that matter, to the Communists of any country. It is one of the ironic aspects of this case that the first people to proclaim their indignation that the President was murdered by the Communists were those who, one day earlier, had been attacking Kennedy as a "pro-Communist" himself, and saying that he was the best friend that the Communists had ever had.

The Communists' responsibility may likewise be excluded on another ground: Assassinations of this type have been committed by the followers of Bakunin, but violence, although approved when socially directed, is opposed to Marxist doctrine when it takes the form of isolated acts of terror. This has been the subject of a long historical debate between the anarchists and Communists. Indeed, in fairness to the anarchists, it must be stated that they are themselves divided on this issue. Marxist policy on vio-

21

lence, by contrast, is defined quite clearly. Acts of terrorism never have been authorized by U. S. Communists under conditions which prevail in their own country. Nor has any Communist in U. S. history been convicted of murder of a government official—or indeed, so far as I am able to determine, any murder or attempted murder. It has thus been necessary for the government, in prosecuting Communists, to charge them not with a specific act of violence nor even with conspiring to commit it, but with a more general offense: under the Smith Act, with "conspiracy to teach and advocate" the Communist form of government, or under the McCarran Act with having failed to register as agents of a foreign government. Evidence to prove the first crime has been limited to showing that defendants read and published certain Marxist books and journals, and attended meetings to discuss the ideas that they had in common. The McCarran Act is also quite remote from acts of violence. It states in its preamble that Communism is a worldwide revolutionary conspiracy, and then requires all persons adhering to such a conspiracy to register as individuals and as a group with the Department of Justice. The Communists thus have the choice of violating this law or, by registering as required, confessing they have violated others—a provision whose constitutionality remains to be clarified.* The most serious crime charged against a Communist in the cold-war period was spying. It was on the charge of espionage, for instance, that the Rosenbergs were executed. But no Communist or person of alleged pro-Communist opinions has been charged, despite the most intense surveillance, of acquiring arms or making an attempt to use them.

* The Supreme Court, on June 8, 1964, upheld a decision of the U. S. Court of Appeals that the 1950 Internal Security Act's compulsory registration feature cannot be enforced, because it violates the Fifth Amendment privilege against self-incrimination.

22

In a situation like the French Resistance, where pacific methods are not in themselves sufficient to achieve a fundamental Communist objective, the assassination of a Fascist leader may be held to serve a social purpose, but the act of murder is not, then, the end—it is a means by which an openly proclaimed objective can be reached. Under such circumstances, Communists do not attempt to hide responsibility for actions they have taken. The United States itself historically takes the same position. U. S. agents during World War II, like those of England and of Russia, were intriguing constantly with discontented Germans in the hope that one of them would murder Hitler.

A rational expression of the Marxist view is that expressed to Jean Daniel by Fidel Castro, when the news came that the President of the United States was dead: "That is bad news, extremely bad news. . . . But tell me, how many Presidents have there been in the United States? Thirty-six? And four of them have been assassinated. That's disturbing. Here in Cuba, there has never been a President assassinated. You know, when we were in the Sierra, there were people (not in my group, but another) who wanted to kill Batista. They believed that they could put an end to the regime by cutting off its head. As for myself, I was always furiously hostile to such methods. First of all, I thought it was politically unrealistic because he would have been replaced by a military chief who would have used the martyrdom of the dictator as an excuse to avenge himself on the revolutionary forces. But I was also opposed to it by temperament because, basically, an assassination of that sort is repugnant to my principles."

If, despite the logic of the international political relations that prevailed after the signing of the Moscow pact, the Communist world revolutionary movement (or a portion of it) had, in fact, judged that the Kennedy assassination would prove beneficial, it could only have been for the reason that they meant to take advantage of the situation, while the government of the United States was in disorganized transition. In this case, the Soviets would have pressed forward with some unilateral solution to the Berlin question; or, in the Pacific, the Chinese might have attacked Formosa. No such incident, in fact, occurred. Both the Chinese and Soviets refrained from all provocative or opportunist action. Thus no benefit, direct or indirect, resulted to the Communists of any nation.

Nowhere but in the United States, accordingly, did the first version of the President's assassination gain a general acceptance. In America, however, the majority of people did believe it. Subtleties of revolutionary ideology are difficult to understand for people who, in all their lives, have never met a Communist or anarchist. It is extremely difficult for them to tell the difference between them. To the average American, moreover, the Pekin-Moscow dispute appears remote. It is as though he heard there was a fight between a hippopotamus and a rhinoceros; he has the feeling that there is a difference between the two, but even if his life depended on it—as, perhaps, it does—he could not tell these animals apart and, since they both seem very large and vicious, he hopes merely that they will contrive to kill each other.

Furthermore, Americans are, on the whole, inclined more readily to trust what they are told officially than Europeans. In no case which I am able to recall, since the McCarthy era, have substantial numbers of the people doubted for a moment that a person said to be a Communist was guilty of whatever crime he had been charged with.

I believe it can be confidently stated that, if Oswald had been brought to trial, not just in Dallas but in any other city in America, he could have been convicted—but on one condition. *Oswald could have been convicted only if he had been innocent.*

But what if he were guilty? What if Oswald knew exactly how the crime had happened? That would be more risky.

*　　　*　　　*

On November 24th, two days after the death of Kennedy, one day after police in Dallas said the case was closed and there was nothing further to investigate, a man named Ruby murdered Oswald in Police Headquarters. He performed this crime, surrounded by policemen who made no attempt to stop him, while the cameras recorded the event before the largest television audience in history. And from that moment, nothing was the same as it had seemed before.

People who were willing to believe that Oswald was a Communist assassin could not be convinced that Ruby was a patriot. It was as simple as that. Average Americans had not had much experience with Oswald's type—a brooding introvert who scarcely even spoke to people. It was hard to say what Oswald might be capable of doing. But they knew Jack Ruby's type quite well. He had his counterparts in every city, men who dealt in anything you wanted—anything that was illegal. Did you like to bet the horses? In America, it's lawful only at the racetrack, but a man like Ruby could take care of you without much trouble. Right across the street there was a pool hall, or perhaps a bowling alley. All you had to do was see a man named Mike, and tell him Tony said it was O.K. Did you like pornographic movies? Or did you prefer the real thing? Just go down to this address, and tell them Tony sent you. Was it marijuana that you needed? Tony knew where you could get it. And if you had parked your car beside a fireplug, Tony would tear up the parking ticket. Tony had a lot of friends in the police; he had to; it was just like paying taxes. Whether it was "Tony" or Jack Ruby, there were thousands like him.

Men like Ruby are well liked by some, and feared by others; they are used by many, like the prostitutes in whom they traffic. But no one believes them when they say that they have shot the President's alleged assassin in a burst of patriotic fervor, to avenge the widow of the martyred leader and spare her the anguish of a "useless trial." Men like Ruby, living in a world of hired assassins, kill for other reasons when they kill. And in the underworld that Ruby had frequented since his childhood, when a witness who is soon to testify in court is murdered, it is for a single purpose: to prevent him from confessing, and from implicating his associates in some crime that has been committed.

Ruby, therefore, must have been involved in some way with the man he slew—such was the general opinion—and no one could conceive of Ruby as a dedicated Communist. The crime which people by the millions witnessed with their own eyes in the living room of their own homes could not be reconciled with any theory the police of Dallas had advanced for Kennedy's assassination.

That, then, was the first conclusion that the public drew. The second was a corollary to it: People who were willing to believe that Oswald carried out his crime unaided could not be convinced that Ruby had no one to help him. Ruby was one of the best-known figures in that border world which lives under continual police surveillance. The police knew him to be aggressive and impulsive, and they knew that he habitually carried weapons. There was no legitimate excuse, at any time, to let a man of that type have free access to Police Headquarters. Still less was it possible to think that, at a moment when the most important prisoner in the United States was being moved, and after Federal police had sent two urgent warnings of a plot to kill him, anyone like Ruby could obtain admittance to the jail, pass through policemen with a loaded gun, unnoticed, and then fire his shot without an effort to restrain him. It had taken place upon the television screen before the eyes of a whole nation, and that nation, for the most part, drew the obvious conclusion.

Some Americans, without believing Ruby's story, were quite pleased that, by his hand, "the Communist assassin got what he deserved." They were such men as, under certain circumstances, join a lynch mob, even if they would not organize it. They were not in the majority, but I would estimate their number to be one-third of the nation.* For wherever there are men like Ruby, there are others who will use them. Men like these do not ask any questions. When they want a girl to spend the night with them or help them win a contract from a client, they pick up the telephone and call a certain number. When they want to bribe a union organizer to avert a strike, they call another. It does not occur to them to wonder who arranges these illegal services or profits from them. Neither did they bother to reflect that Ruby, whom they cheered, and Oswald, whom they hated, might have both been playing for the same team.

For the most part, though, Americans rejected Ruby as a symbol of their Way of Life—though as a Way of Death his mission was accomplished in the best tradition of our gangster pictures. Much, of course, was written of the lurid aspect of his Dallas enterprises, fronts for his more serious activity—of his stripteaser Tammi True, the star of a burlesque house called the Carousel, who asks the

* In March, 1964, the National Opinion Research Center of the University of Chicago said a survey it had just completed showed 11 percent of the U. S. population had hoped that the President's assassin would be shot or lynched. I am inclined to think that for each citizen that would admit it, there are probably two more who would be reluctant to disclose this feeling.

27

customers to verify by hand that they have not been cheated; of the "amateur" performances where, one reporter said, the female customers were coaxed with prizes to outstrip each other. That is unimportant. But when this man, who for two days mingled with reporters, jovial and smiling, passing out his calling cards in black and pink, "the color of the underwear of his performers," suddenly proclaimed himself the champion of Kennedy's young widow, whom he called by her first name—that was the ultimate obscenity which most Americans could not forgive him.

Most responsible reporters now began requestioning the theses that they had accepted. They observed, to their dismay, that there had been a general default by the police and by the press itself, a failure to give Oswald the protection, physical and verbal, to which he was legally entitled. On the day after the second murder, *The New York Times* declared:

> The Dallas authorities, abetted and encouraged by the newspaper, TV and radio press, trampled on every principle of justice in their handling of Lee H. Oswald. It is their sworn duty to protect every prisoner, as well as the community, and to afford each accused person full opportunity for his defense before a properly constituted court. . . . Yet —before any indictment had been returned or any evidence presented, in the face of continued denials by the prisoner— the chief of police and the district attorney pronounced Oswald guilty. "Basically, the case is closed," the chief declared. . . . After two days of such pre-findings of guilt, in an electrically emotional atmosphere . . . the jail transfer was made at high noon and with the widest possible advance announcement. It was an outrageous breach of police responsibility—no matter what the demands of reporters and cameramen may have been—to move Oswald in public under circumstances in which he could so easily have been the victim of attack.

A suspect, under Anglo-Saxon common law, not only has the right to physical protection but to a judicial process which was not observed—the right to be considered innocent until a court has found him guilty. With considerable dignity and courage, *The New York Times,* on November 27th, carried a signed statement by its managing editor, Turner Catledge, in which he acknowledged that the *Times* had "erred" in calling Oswald, without any qualifying phrase, the "President's assassin" in a front-page headline. "Under the American system of justice," Catledge noted, "he is innocent until proved guilty. Future articles and headlines will reflect that fact."

Once doubt of such proportions in the first official version of the Kennedy assassination was implanted, the whole thesis of a Communist conspiracy began to undergo a transformation. It did not completely disappear; it merely faded. It was pointed out that no one had contended Oswald had accomplices; it was quite certain that he had none, the police insisted. The director of the F.B.I., J. Edgar Hoover, said there was no basis to believe that U. S. Communists had been involved in Oswald's plot in any way.

But since no one retracted any element of the large mass of evidence which the police of Dallas had accumulated and which, federal police investigators subsequently said, proved Oswald's guilt completely, how was this discrepancy to be explained? For it seemed scarcely credible that a pro-Communist would kill the President of the United States without consulting any left-wing group or individual, and for no motive that they would approve—for most observers in the U. S. now agreed with what the foreign press had said from the beginning: Oswald's act had done the Communists a great disservice.

Why would any Communist, in short, behave as though he were an anti-Communist?

29

There seemed to be just one solution: It was only possible if he were crazy. So each day the emphasis was shifted more and more in this direction: Oswald had been a deranged fanatic. And miraculously, it was found that Ruby, too, was crazy—temporarily, of course. It was assumed that, once his innocence had been pronounced in court, his sanity would be restored to him as suddenly as it had disappeared. But his attorneys said that the much-vaunted patriotic frenzy which had struck him just before he fired the shot at Oswald had been nothing but a brief attack of mental illness—a distressing incident of which he now remembered nothing.

Thus the second version of the double murder was that neither of the two assassins had a reasonable motive. It was not a patriotic citizen who killed a Communist assassin to avenge the widow of the President; it was one madman who shot down another.

*   *   *

To those citizens who, in their innocence, believe Jack Ruby's version of the motives that impelled him, I can only urge them to return to reading comic books, for history will merely bore them. It is history which we must now consult, however, for the argument advanced by those who think Oswald was crazy is essentially that in all previous assassinations which have taken place in the United States, the President's assassin was a madman.

There has been no scientific demonstration that the suspect, Oswald, had been suffering a mental illness that provoked the crime. The only evidence to this effect was ludicrously inconclusive—a report that, as a schoolboy, a psychiatrist examined him and found alarming symptoms

30

that he was not properly adjusted. During Oswald's adult life, particularly during his three years of military service, any tendency toward insanity would certainly have been detected. *Time* reported on November 29th, "Various neighbors, past and present, described him as seeming reasonably intelligent, although generally silent to the point of acting contemptuous." The associate pastor of First Unitarian Church in Dallas, Rev. Byrd Helligas, told the Washington *Post* on December 1st that Oswald was "calm" and gave no indication of any "frustration." Roy S. Truly, Oswald's last employer, said, "He seemed just a normal, quiet young fellow." Oswald's conduct, as observed by news reporters after his arrest, seemed altogether normal, even after he had been subjected to two days of the most severe emotional and physical tension. And the Dallas district attorney, Henry Wade, when asked while Oswald was still living if there was a chance that he was crazy, categorically denied it.

The whole argument thus rests upon the feeling which most people have that an assassin, by the very nature of his crime, must be insane—that is to say, that the enormity of such an act precludes the possibility of any reasonable motive.

It is evident that such a theory would be quite attractive to a lawyer undertaking the defense of an assassin. Some attorneys who have had this duty, after the assassination of a President of the United States, have hinted that their client was a madman. One defendant tried, by his behavior in the courtroom, to make his attorney's argument appear convincing. He was executed, like the others. Legally, so far as Presidential murders are concerned, the argument that an assassination can take place without a reasonable motive has not ever gained acceptance, in default of proof that the accused had demonstrated by his previous behavior that he was psychotic.

Mere acceptance of political beliefs which the majority of people would repudiate is not, of course, an indication of insanity, whose classic legal definition is the inability to understand the consequences of one's acts. Each previous assassin has been held to know what he was doing; each one had a real, not an imaginary, grievance; each expected that the crime would benefit the group that he belonged to; and in each case, the assassin was a member of the party which was most fanatically hostile to the policies the President had been pursuing at the time that he was murdered.

It must be remembered that whenever there is bitter civil disagreement, a large number of the people feel their country's interests would be advanced if leaders of the opposition could be silenced, and there is no need to cite examples in the recent history of Germany or Spain in order to sustain this thesis. In a civil conflict, one side's hero is the other's "tyrant" or "fanatic," and the murderer of Hitler would have been regarded as a brave and lucid man by the United Nations.

History reflects, in large degree, the verdict of the victors, and that judgment often has been that the victim was insane, not the assassin. Such, for instance, is the general opinion of Caligula, the young man who, at twenty-five, became the Emperor of Rome and for eight months was noted for his mildness and his acts of justice. Following an illness, though, Caligula embarked upon a three-year reign of terror, taking a delight in spectacles of torture; had himself declared a god, and built himself a temple; elevated his horse, Incitatus, to the rank of consul; and was finally struck down by officers of his own guard. No court today would have declared Caligula's assassins to have been insane.

But what is one to say of Caesar, and of Brutus? Each man had supporters who believed sincerely that their adversary was insane with the ambition to acquire new power.

The debate on this point has continued through the ages.

John Wilkes Booth, the first man to assassinate a President of the United States, thought Lincoln was a tyrant who deserved to die, like Caesar. The first words Booth uttered after he performed the act were those attributed to Brutus when the Roman Emperor had fallen—"Sic semper tyrannis" (Thus may tyrants always die), which had a dual meaning, since it happened equally to be the motto of Virginia, the capital of the Confederacy to which Booth professed allegiance.

Booth, of course, was thought by many to have been a madman. Tales were told, after the crime was known, of aspects of Booth's character which lent a certain plausibility to this suspicion. He was said to have been subject to attacks of sudden anger out of all proportion to the insult he imagined he had suffered. Once, discussing politics with members of his family, Booth leaped up and grabbed his sister's husband by the throat to strangle him. His sensitivity derived, according to most explanations, from the fact that he had been the last and least successful of America's most celebrated family of actors. Junius Brutus Booth, his father, came to the United States in 1821 from England, where he had already been considered one of the most gifted of contemporary actors, starring in the roles of Shakespeare. Edwin Thomas Booth, the elder son of Junius, achieved fame in both countries on the stage, especially for his appearances in *Hamlet*. John Wilkes Booth, the younger, was indeed eclipsed by these two, but it is completely false to think of him as an obscure, untalented and unemployed actor. He was well known and in demand in his profession, not just for the name he bore but for his own good looks and air of smoldering, romantic passion.

There were, it is true, more elements of melodrama than efficient and cold-blooded murder in the manner in which the assassination was accomplished. Booth shot Lincoln

33

while the President was sitting in a theatre box in Washington, watching a play. Five days before, with the surrender of the Southern armies under Lee, the Civil War had come to its conclusion. After Booth had fired one bullet into Lincoln's brain, he lingered on the scene, although he could have made his exit swiftly and discreetly through a theatre with whose passageways he was familiar. Nor did Booth shoot the one man who was in a position to arrest him. The assassin chose, instead, to stab him in the arm, using a knife he had been holding in his other hand. Then he rushed past the dying President, the wounded officer beside him and two frightened women, put his left hand on the railing of the box and vaulted down upon the stage, where all this time the play had been continuing. It was a long drop, but no higher than the rocks from which the lithe young actor frequently had made his entrance scene, as in Macbeth's encounter with the witches. It would not have been beyond his physical ability, had all gone as he had expected. But, as Booth jumped down, the spur of one boot caught upon the flag with which the presidential box was draped—the Union flag, which Booth so hated. Thus Booth's leg was twisted underneath him, and he fell upon it. It was later learned the leg was actually broken, but Booth rose and, turning to the audience, many of whom recognized him and assumed his leap had some connection with the comedy that they were watching, raised his bloody knife and cried, "Sic semper tyrannis!" Then he limped rapidly across the stage and vanished. Two or three men, hearing the commotion in the presidential box, rose from their seats and started to run after Booth. He reached the exit, leaped upon a horse which had been waiting for him and rode off before pursuers could be organized to chase him. It was not until eleven days had passed that he was found in Bowling Green, Virginia, hiding on a farm behind the Southern lines, where he had fled. Refusing to sur-

34

render, Booth was shot down by one of the men who had been ordered to effect his capture. He died there, three hours later.

Was the man insane? Well, certainly there is more evidence of mental instability in John Wilkes Booth than in the two men thus far linked with Kennedy's assassination, and if Booth had carried out his plan and his escape in total isolation, it might now be possible to give more weight to the first popular reaction, "Only a demented mind could possibly have done that."

But was Booth alone? For the hypothesis of an insane assassin can at once be shelved the moment that it can be shown that he did not commit, or could not have committed his assassination unless some accomplice had assisted him. Conspiracy implies a motive. It is not conceivable that two insane assassins could cooperate to kill the President of the United States. The possibility, already infinitely small, diminishes still further if the plot extends to three or more conspirators.

This does not, certainly, preclude the chance that a demented or moronic person can be used in such a crime. Conceivably—although it is less likely—he may even be assigned the murder role. But in the plot which John Wilkes Booth directed, he preferred to fire the fatal shot himself although, among his followers, there were two men who, if subjected to a modern psychiatric test, would probably be judged psychotic.

The mere fact that he had managed to escape the searching parties sent to chase him, and contrived, despite his injured leg, to hide eleven days before they caught him, would have been sufficient reason to suspect that Booth was not alone. He had accomplices and sympathizers. There was no necessity to wait eleven days, however. The extensive aims of the conspiracy became at once apparent. Lincoln had not been the only target on the night of April

14, 1865. The three top leaders of the government had all been destined for a simultaneous assassination. Each, of course, was to have had a separate assassin.

Lincoln had been shot a little after 10 P.M. Two hours earlier, the man who shot him had entrusted to the hands of an associate a small, wrapped package. The two men compared their watches. And precisely at the moment Booth was entering the theatre, his associate was riding up on horseback to the private home of Lincoln's Secretary of State.

The name of the young man upon the horse was Lewis Thornton Powell. He had come originally from the Southern state of Florida and fought, at one time, in the Southern army. (Booth himself had seen no bullet fired in battle, though he was of military age and in good health. Despite his fervor for the Southern cause, he had continued acting.) Powell had assumed the name of "Payne." He was a man of an extraordinary strength, and he was mentally deficient. He was thus the perfect instrument for executing any brutal crime in which he did not have to do much thinking. The plan which he was meant to execute had been conceived by Booth, by whom he had, for some time, been instructed in his duties. Powell would have been incapable of formulating such a plan himself and, once required to use his own initiative, he was not mentally equipped to make the right adjustment to developments which had not been anticipated by the man from whom he took his orders.

The behavior of Powell is, accordingly, instructive. It may be assumed that any effort at assassination by an isolated madman would present the same, or even more, insuperable obstacles. For Powell had the great advantage, at the outset, of a plan to follow—of a clever, reasonable plan, prepared by a malign but reasonable human being. A lone madman would not have this impetus to help him.

William H. Seward, Secretary of State and, next to Lincoln, the key figure in the government, was lying in his bed when Powell rode up to the door. A few days earlier, the carriage in which Seward had been riding had an accident, and he was thrown in such a way that his right arm and jaw were fractured. Booth had learned of this, and planned to take advantage of it. Powell, following instructions, leaped down from his horse and rushed up to the house. Beneath his arm, he had the package Booth had given him. He told the servant at the door that it was medicine the doctor who had been attending Seward had instructed him to bring the patient. When the servant offered to deliver it, the "messenger" replied that it was urgent and that his instructions were to give it to the nurse directly. Powell forced his way inside the house and started up the stairs. The servant followed him, protesting, and the sound of their dissension brought the Secretary's son into the hall to settle the disturbance. Frederick W. Seward was a leading government official in his own right—the Assistant Secretary of State. He said that he would personally take the package to his father. Powell had not been prepared to deal with any intervention by a member of the family; the answers that had been composed for him were valid only in disposing of the servant. He reflected for a moment. Then he drew his pistol and rushed blindly at the man who had been interfering with his mission. Powell pulled the trigger. It misfired the first time that he tried to use it, so he beat his victim on the head with it until they fell, together, through the doorway of the Secretary's room. The Secretary's son lay on the floor, unconscious, and remained for weeks in a coma.

In the sickroom, by the Secretary's bed, there was his daughter and a male nurse from the medical corps of the army. Both of them were hurled aside by Powell, and the nurse fell with a knife wound. Powell then began to strike the target that had been selected for him. He stabbed Seward deeply three times in the cheek and neck. The Secretary, trying to escape him, fell between the bed and the adjoining wall. The male nurse had by this time struggled to his feet and, seizing the assassin from behind, pulled him away from Seward's bedside. Powell turned upon the man and stabbed him twice more in the shoulder. Meanwhile, Seward's other son, Augustus, who was now a colonel in the army, came in answer to his sister's screams, seized Powell and, although severely wounded in the head and face, contrived to push him through the bedroom doorway. As he fled, another servant tried to stop him. Powell left him seriously wounded and ran out of the door, unhurt, riding to safety on the horse which he, like Booth, had left outside the building. He hid in the woods near Washington and seemed to have escaped completely, but he was so helpless without Booth to guide him that he came back two days later to the little town, Surrattsville, Maryland, where he expected to receive additional instructions. The police were at that very moment questioning the owner of the tavern where, it was suspected, Booth and other plotters had been meeting. It was owned by Mary E. Surratt, a widow, member of a family that, as might be suspected, had been influential in Surrattsville, but her former wealth was gone and she had been reduced to operation of a boarding-house and tavern—which apparently she felt to be "beneath" her. When police asked Powell if he knew her, he replied that he was working for her. But the widow, unaware of his reply but fearing Powell had confessed already, raised her right hand and, with all the piety of Southern gentlewomen, solemnly declared, "Before God, I do not know him, never saw him, and never hired him." That extraordinary falsehood was interpreted correctly as an indication that they shared the secret of the President's assassination, and they both were hanged as Booth's accomplices on July 7, 1865. The tavern owner, evidence revealed, had played no passive role in the conspiracy; she had not only furnished quarters for the plotters but participated in their preparations for the murder and, with the assistance of her son and an employee whom she hired to run the tavern, actually furnished Booth with weapons.*

When a military board had finished its investigation of the President's assassination, two more men were hanged with Powell and the lady from Surrattsville. One of these, David E. Herold, was a druggist's clerk. Like Powell, he was probably a moron, but his character was much less brutal; his chief role was to accompany his leader, Booth, on his escape into Virginia, helping him find food and shelter, guarding him when he was sleeping. To imagine him as the unaided murderer of Lincoln is, on any close investigation of his nature, totally beyond consideration.

The fourth plotter who was hung was German-born George Atzerodt, a spy for the Confederacy, who had promised to kill Andrew Johnson, the Vice-President. This was the only element in Booth's conspiracy which failed completely. Atzerodt appears to have had difficulty summoning the necessary courage, but the court, in passing sentence, took due recognition of the fact that murder had been his intention

Three more men—the doctor who hid Booth and helped him to escape, and two secession advocates from Maryland who took part in the preparation for the crimes in meetings in Surrattsville—were condemned for life for a complicity involving less direct participation. The life sentences were later shortened. A scene shifter at Ford's Theatre was condemned to jail for six years. John M. Lloyd, the tavern keeper hired by Mary E. Surratt, was deeply implicated in the plot, but he escaped the punishment he merited by

* Details of the conspiracy based chiefly on *Abraham Lincoln*, by Nicolay and Hay, one of the chief classical biographies.

giving the police the information which led them to the headquarters of the plotters. It was not the first time Lloyd had been in contact with the agents of the law. The tavern job was just a front for his real occupation—smuggling contraband across the border. With his connections with the underworld he would, in modern times, be called a gangster. It is interesting, therefore, to observe the chain of Booth's conspiracy snapped at its weakest link—its mercenary member.

One conspirator, John H. Surratt, the tavern owner's son, contrived to cross the border into Canada, where he was hidden by a monastery and, in time, went on to Europe to become a member of the Papal Zouaves. By the time Surratt was found and brought to trial in 1867, the whole atmosphere of the United States had changed. The public indignation of the first few months had dulled. Incredible as it may seem, it was impossible to get a jury to convict Surratt. The jurors were divided, and he was acquitted.

Thus, the popular opinion that the murderer of Lincoln must have been insane, and carried out his crime unaided, had turned out to be a false one. For not only did Booth have accomplices below, he also had accomplices above him. These accomplices were never punished. They escaped the scaffold through the fact that the one man who could have implicated them was silenced. That one man was John Wilkes Booth—and Booth himself was murdered while, like Lee H. Oswald, he was in the custody of men who had arrested him.

The murderer of Lincoln had been sleeping in a barn with Herold, his deranged young helper, when they were aroused by sounds of the approach of the arresting party. The lieutenant, E. P. Doherty, who led these men, called out to Booth and Herold to surrender, threatening to set fire to the barn if they did not obey his ultimatum. Herold then came rushing out but Booth, too proud to let himself be captured until he had played his role to the last moment of dramatic value, lingered while the flames were kindled. Then, when he was clearly visible in the tobacco barn, outlined against the light, and at a time when he was not attempting to escape, a sergeant in the party, disobeying orders to bring Booth back to stand trial, fired at the prisoner, who died three hours later. Booth, during this time, was conscious but unable to communicate with those around him and, if he had any last confession, boast, or angry accusation, was unable to express it.

This was certainly a stroke of fortune for the men Booth might have implicated. When the trial of the minor members of the plot took place, their secondary role was clearly stressed by U. S. Government attorneys. The chief plotters had not yet been captured. Foremost of them was no less than Jefferson Davis, President of the Confederacy, and a reward of $100,000 was offered for his arrest, *uniquely on this charge of being an accessory to murder,* and quite apart from all the other crimes of treason which he had committed. The official charges brought by the United States against those members of the plot who had been caught accused them of "maliciously, unlawfully and traitorously . . . combining, confederating and conspiring with one John H. Surratt, John Wilkes Booth, Jefferson Davis, George N. Sanders, Beverly Tucker, Jacob Thompson, William C. Cleary, Clement C. Clay, George Harper, George Young and others unknown to kill and murder . . . Abraham Lincoln . . . Andrew Johnson . . . William H. Seward . . . and Ulysses S. Grant. . . ."

Even in the absence of the government's key witness, Booth, the U. S. prosecutors proved that the Ford's Theatre plot was not, as had been first supposed, a sudden impulse born of the desire for vengeance after Lee surrendered. The conspiracy was of at least a year's duration and in its original conception it had been a military operation, not an isolated act of terror. Booth had planned to capture Lincoln, not to kill him. He then planned, with the assistance of his own group and of other Southern sympathizers, to transport the President behind the Southern lines, where he would be delivered to the government of the Confederacy. Booth had gone to Canada, and there discussed this project with Confederate agents, including ultimately Jacob Thompson, the personal emissary of Jefferson Davis and probably the most important representative of the Confederate regime in Canada, which had, throughout the war, been the chief center of intrigue between Confederate agents and Northern traitors. Thompson, who had been Minister of the Interior in the pro-Southern administration of President Buchanan, who preceded Lincoln, was sufficiently impressed by Booth's proposal that he transferred funds to his account in the Ontario Bank in Montreal; a check effecting this transfer of funds was produced in evidence by John A. Bingham, Special Judge Advocate before the military commission which tried the plotters. After securing this official approval and tangible evidence of the Confederate Government's support, Booth returned to the United States to recruit the people he would need to help him to accomplish his objective. It was noticed by his friends that he seemed, in the latter part of 1864, to be unusually well equipped with money. He explained to them that he had made it speculating in oil stocks, but at the trial Booth's broker testified that Booth had never made a penny from that source; that, on the contrary, his gambling on the stock exchange had been disastrous.

When the Southern armies were defeated and surrender loomed, the group that Booth had gathered for the kidnap plot assumed that it would have to be abandoned. They had not yet found the opportunity to capture Lincoln; he was too well guarded. Now it seemed to be too late, and one conspirator wrote Booth a letter, eighteen days before the

President was killed, expressing this conviction. He suggested that, before proceeding further, Booth himself should "go and see how it will be taken in Richmond." From the implications of this letter and from other testimony, it seems evident that Booth had kept the Southern capital informed of his activities through agents sent behind the Northern lines to see him; and that, far from being the sole instigator of the plot, he was no more than a lieutenant, subject to the orders of conspirators above him, whose authority he had continued to respect until the fall of the Confederacy had removed this obligation. If the final murderous expression of the plot was Booth's own formulation, as appears most likely, the responsibility for the original conspiracy extends to circles far above him—to respectable and honored men like Jacob Thompson, and so directly to the capital of the Confederacy and its rulers.

This point was made clear by Special Judge Advocate Bingham, after producing the check marked "Pay to order of J. Wilkes Booth" and identifying the writer of the check, under the signature, as "agent of Jefferson Davis." "What more is wanting?" asked the U. S. Government prosecutor. "Surely no word further need be spoken to show that . . . Jefferson Davis and his several agents, named in Canada, were in this conspiracy. If any additional evidence is wanting to show the complicity of Davis in it let the paper found in the possession of the hired assassin Booth come to bear witness against him."

Were Davis and the other Confederate leaders morally incapable of such an act as murder (for, as in any kidnap plot, the threat of murder was implicit)?

Evidence proves they were not above it. On file in the office of the Judge Advocate General in Washington, a letter found in the Confederate Archives reveals that a Lieutenant Alston of the Southern army wrote to President Jefferson Davis in 1864, at the same time Booth was in

43

contact with Canadian agents of the Southern states. Alston proposed to organize a plot for Lincoln's murder which, he said, "would rid his country of some of her deadliest enemies by striking at the very heart's blood of those who seek to enchain her in slavery." Davis ordered the proposal to be thoroughly investigated to find out if Alston's project had a good chance of succeeding. So the murder offer went, by Davis' direction, to the office of the Secretary of War, where the Assistant Secretary gave it his own personal examination and referred it to the Adjutant General, marked "for attention."

It seems clear that Lincoln's murder was considered a potential, practical objective of the Southern states, whose highest leaders ordered such proposals to be studied and, if sound, encouraged by supplying funds to the conspirators; that there were, consequently, many groups like Booth's throughout the North, each operating independently of one another; that if any of them had attempted to perform their mission and had been arrested, they would probably have been repudiated, as is customary when a spy or saboteur has been detected.

None of this, however, could be proved beyond all possibility of doubt, once the assassin had himself been murdered. All the trails between the rebel government and Lincoln's murder passed through Booth—and Booth had been forever silenced. He could never be examined as a witness, and the man who shot him, Boston Corbett, brooded on this fact until he spent the last part of his life in an insane asylum. The defendants tried for Lincoln's death were simple executioners of a conspiracy whose authors were, apart from Booth himself, not punished. Theodore Roscoe, writing the preface to *The Web of Conspiracy*, concludes: "The facts indicate that the criminals responsible for Lincoln's death got away with murder."

Davis was, of course, eventually arrested, under circumstances which, for such a proud man, had been painfully humiliating. He was caught while fleeing the advancing Northern armies with his family, his servants and his portable possessions, hoping to escape by boat from Florida to Texas. Rumors reached him that a gang of his own soldiers, recently disbanded, was preparing to attack his wagon train to rob him, having heard that he was carrying away a portion of the Southern gold reserves. The Northern troops, however, were the first to reach him. Coming to the tent where Davis hid, the soldiers had been met by Mrs. Davis, who came out barefooted, put her hand upon the first man's arm, and murmured, blushing, that he must not enter, for her daughter was in no condition to receive male guests. After a little while, Miss Maggie Howell (who was not her daughter, but her sister) came out of the tent. Beside her was a lady bent with age and carrying a pail. The bent old lady had a shawl around her head. She told the soldiers that she had to go down to the stream; she said that it was urgent; she implored them please to stand aside and let her pass. The soldiers hesitated. Mrs. Davis was indignant and, with an aristocratic manner, cried, "For God's sake, let my old mother go to get some water!" They stood back, then, and the poor old lady hobbled off toward the woods. But as she walked, some of the soldiers noticed that, for one of her apparent age and sex, she had extremely heavy boots on, and a corporal rode up behind her, ordering her to remove her shawl. Exposed, the man in feminine attire turned out to be the missing President of the Confederacy, who was so enraged at having made himself ridiculous that he began denouncing all his captors, saying it was shameful for them to be searching women. "Is there a man among you? If there is," he cried out, "let me see him!"

"Yes, I am one, and if you stir," the corporal who had arrested him retorted, "I will blow your brains out!" There was very little trouble with the President of the Confederacy after that.*

Arrest, however, did not mean conviction. Davis was not even prosecuted for conspiracy to murder. With the death of Lincoln, the whole climate of the country quickly changed. Men who only a few years earlier had fought against their country were once more installed in power. Several of the witnesses who had appeared in court to link the name of Jefferson Davis directly to the plot of Booth decided, one year later, it would be more prudent to retract their statements. Davis spent two years, delicately treated, in a Southern prison; was at last indicted for the crime of treason. But the charge was brought before a court in Richmond, capital of the Confederacy, and Virginia judges were unable to agree on a decision. The whole matter was referred to the U. S. Supreme Court. While the case was pending, amnesty for all the Southern prisoners was given by the President of the United States, a Southerner named Johnson, who had been Vice-President when Lincoln had been slain, and who had been the only one of the three top officials to escape unharmed from the planned triple murder. In the months which followed Lincoln's murder, Johnson was among the loudest in demanding vengeance; later, though, his ardor cooled, and he became associated so overtly with the Southern opposition to the policies of Reconstruction that a vote was taken in the Senate to impeach him which, if passed, would have removed him from

* Davis himself, after long years of rancor and reflection, wrote a somewhat nobler version of his conduct in his book, *Rise and Fall of the Confederate Government*. He says that it was so dark in the tent that he picked up his wife's coat, put it on by accident, and she then thoughtfully gave him her shawl, "the morning being damp and chilly." He maintains that when the corporal told him to stop, he gave him a "defiant answer," threw away his wife's coat and her shawl, and would have thrown the fellow off his horse and ridden off upon it if his wife had not, at that decisive moment, thrown her arms around him. By a series of misfortunes of this sort, the Civil War was lost.

46

his office—something which has never happened in the history of the United States. There had been 35 votes to impeach the President and 19 votes in his support; but since impeachment is effective only by two-thirds majority, one vote was lacking. A new President had already been elected and was waiting to take office when, at Christmas, 1868, Johnson proclaimed, "unconditionally and without reservation, to all and to every person who directly or indirectly participated in the late insurrection or rebellion, a full pardon and amnesty for the offense of treason against the United States, or of adhering to their enemies, during the late civil war, with restoration of all rights, privileges, and immunities, under the Constitution and the laws which have been made in pursuance thereof."

Davis already had been freed on bail, a large part of which was provided by one of the country's richest men, the Northern millionaire, Cornelius Vanderbilt. Business-as-usual was the country's mood; to fix responsibility for Lincoln's death seemed now a matter better left for the historians to argue; "no good purpose could be served" by asking questions likely to embarrass Southerners whose help was needed for the Reconstruction.

After the amnesty, all charges pending against Davis were dismissed. He lived for twenty-one more years, dying in 1889, almost a quarter of a century after the death of Lincoln, news of whose assassination, read to Southern troops as Davis stood before them, had been greeted with wild cheers of exultation—"as was natural," wrote Davis later, "at news of the fall of one whom they considered their most powerful foe. . . . For an enemy so relentless, in the war for our subjugation, we could not be expected to mourn." *

What part in the first assassination of the President of

* Davis, op. cit.

the United States can be explained by mental illness, as that term is understood in a contemporary courtroom? None. Among the group which Booth assembled, two men were of such subnormal levels of intelligence that they may properly be classified as mentally deranged. But neither could have carried out even his own share of the plot in isolation. Men of this type can be used as instruments in an assassination, but they cannot organize it. They are capable of wholesale carnage of the type inflicted on the Seward family by Powell, but for crimes requiring foresight and ability to vary tactics in accordance with a changing situation, they are useless.

This, however, does not mean the murder of the President cannot be carried out by a deranged man of a higher mental order, but the courts of the United States have held that this insanity must have a pattern recognizable by a physician. The prevailing precedent that governs is the one established in the case of Charles J. Guiteau, who was executed for the shots he fired at James A. Garfield, second President of the United States to die by an assassin's bullet. Garfield had been shot on July 2, 1881, only a few months after taking office. His assassin was at once arrested and immediately made a full confession which, months later, was retracted when his lawyer pleaded the defendant was deranged, and therefore could not properly be punished.

Guiteau was himself a lawyer—or, at least, aspired to be one—and, like many men in that profession, hoped for a political career. In the election which took place in 1880, Guiteau had been thwarted. He had cast his lot with the wrong faction in his party and, though the Republicans had been elected, the rewards were being given to the men who had backed Garfield in his fight for nomination at the last Republican convention. Guiteau's faction, the New York group which was called the Stalwarts, had been Garfield's chief opponents. Guiteau, at the age of thirty-nine, was still a minor politician and an unsuccessful lawyer. It is hardly likely that the candidate he had supported would have given him the favor that he asked—a minor diplomatic post in France. Still less did Garfield, with whom he incessantly demanded interviews. Garfield ignored him, being at the time besieged by other office seekers like him. Finally, in anger and frustration, Guiteau took a pistol and went down to the railroad station where the President—one of the gentlest and most intellectual men ever to have held that office—was preparing to leave Washington for a brief visit to the university he had attended. The enraged attorney shouted at him as he raised his pistol, and fired twice toward him. One shot grazed the arm of Garfield and the wound was superficial, but the other lodged inside him near the spine and he was taken to the hospital in grave condition. Garfield struggled to recover from his wound all summer, but he finally succumbed to its effects September 19th.

Guiteau had a motive for his action. It was not the crime of an insane man who strikes out against his victim blindly, and without a reason. Guiteau hated Garfield; he believed the President had thwarted him and others like him of rewards to which they were entitled for their service to their party. He thought Garfield had accepted their support in the election but, once in the White House, had appointed only anti-Stalwart politicians to the various administrative jobs which were traditionally given to the men who worked the hardest for the winning party. He was not insane but angry, moved by the desire for vengeance. If all murderers who have been similarly motivated were to be declared insane, the crime of murder would be rarely punished.

An insane man, thinking only of the persecution he imagined he had suffered at the hands of Garfield, would have made some reference to this supposed injustice as he took his vengeance. Guiteau had a more sophisticated formulation of his motive. Sane men usually do, when they commit an act which, even to themselves, would seem intolerably petty or ignoble if they dared admit it. They invent a nobler reason, and deceive themselves with the belief that they are acting for a group that has been wronged, not for themselves alone. And so Guiteau proclaimed triumphantly as he shot Garfield, that with Garfield dead, Vice-President Chester A. Arthur would become the President, and Arthur was a Stalwart!

This was not the raving of a lunatic's delusions. The assassination did, indeed, transfer the power to the group Guiteau supported. Garfield, having won the nomination for the Presidency in a bitter fight, had tried to make peace in his party by at once requesting the defeated faction to name their man as Vice-Presidential candidate; and so, as often happens in the U.S.A., the two top leaders of the country represented fundamentally opposing views. This had been true of Andrew Johnson, under Lincoln, and it was to be true in the 1960 Democratic National Convention, in which Kennedy chose as his running mate the candidate whom he had just defeated. Three times out of four, so far, the murdered President of the United States has been succeeded by a man selected by his right-wing opposition. In the fourth case, as will be apparent, President McKinley, though himself of the extreme right, was succeeded by an even more extreme right-winger.

Where Guiteau miscalculated—and it merely shows that he was an atrocious politician, not that he was mentally deranged—was in expecting that his act would be a good thing for the Stalwarts *if he openly avowed his loyalty to that group.* He had been prepared to risk his own life, as he sacrificed the life of Garfield, for what he described as a "political necessity" which would "unite the party." In a letter written in advance of the assassination and produced by Guiteau at the time that he was seized, he asked the leaders of the Stalwart faction to provide protection for him. He described himself as a "Stalwart of Stalwarts," citing work that he had done in the campaign for Stalwart candidates.

Guiteau supposed the death of Garfield would produce the same effect as had the death of Lincoln. Similar considerations of political expediency, in Lincoln's time, induced the President's own party, in the 1864 elections, to propose a Southerner who had been loyal to the Union as the candidate for the Vice-Presidency. Actually, Johnson was a Democrat and Lincoln a Republican, but since the Civil War was still in progress the Republicans had merged their forces temporarily with those men in the Democratic Party who opposed secession of the Southern states, in which the Democrats traditionally had their strength. The combination for the 1864 campaign was called the Union Party. Andrew Johnson was the only Southern Congressman who had stayed loyal to the Union. He courageously had risked assassination, speaking in defense of loyalty to the United States in Tennessee, his native state, where other "Yankee sympathizers" were, by this time, being killed or beaten. The first term in which Lincoln had been elected in 1860, the Vice-President had been a native of the state of Maine, it being felt that with a Westerner like Lincoln as the Presidential candidate, the second post should be awarded to an Easterner. Lincoln had frequently said jokingly that he was not in danger of being assassinated, since his Vice-President was known to be an even more implacable foe of the Confederacy than he was himself. In 1864, however, it seemed more astute to show the South that even Southerners were welcome to hold major posts in the Union Government, provided they were willing to be loyal to it.

Johnson had not been a major figure in the government while Lincoln lived. He was completely overshadowed, not alone by Lincoln but by members of the Cabinet as well.

Among these men, most of whom had been educated in the large northeastern schools and universities, he felt himself to be a simple country boy. He certainly was not an intellectual; of all men who have ever occupied the White House, Johnson had least education. He had been illiterate until he married. At an early age he entered politics, and won his first election at the age of twenty-one. He ultimately worked his way up in the ranks of his own party until he was made the Governor of Tennessee, and also served as an obscure member of Congress. His political career was marked by inconsistent views; he fought the rich landowners on some questions, urging higher taxes and free public education, but was a convinced supporter of their interests when slavery became the issue. His opinions were, in general, those of a self-made man and his experience was largely that of life not far from the frontier.

Being a simple man, Johnson was shocked by the assassination and his first reaction was to make sure Booth's conspirators were punished with the maximum severity. He was too lacking in sophistication, probably, to draw the necessary inferences from the plot, to understand completely the extent to which the origin of the conspiracy, and others like it which had not succeeded, was the President of the Confederacy and his various assistants. So the lesser members of the plot were punished—some, like Herold and the doctor who had treated Booth's leg, with undue severity. But the real authors of the whole conspiracy remained exempt from justice. After the first public passion to avenge the President had died, the differences which divided Johnson from the Northerners grew more and more apparent. He opposed the Congress on the fundamental issues of the period of reconstruction. Congress wanted the new Negro citizens to have the right to vote, but Johnson said the Southern states (who were, of course, opposed to that) should be permitted to decide the question. Congress passed a bill appropriating money to the former slaves to help them while they searched for work; the President refused to sign it. Congress tried to bar men who had fought against their government from holding office until 1870; the President, in 1868, gave them an amnesty.

Guiteau believed the same thing would take place if Garfield were eliminated, and to some extent it did. Of all the men whom Garfield had selected for his Cabinet—the men who otherwise would have controlled the country for the next four years—only one man was not replaced by Arthur. That exception was a man he dared not touch— the son of Lincoln. On the other hand, however, the new President broke with the Stalwarts also. The overt admission that the murderer had acted as their agent had the opposite effect to what Guiteau expected. Garfield's gallant fight for life drew the whole nation's sympathy toward him; at the same time, public hatred of the Stalwarts drove their candidates from office. Roscoe Conkling, the chief Stalwart leader, was defeated in a bid for re-election to the Senate only a few days after Garfield had been shot. He had been the unchallenged boss of the corrupt New York political machine, notorious for stealing public funds and for its close links with the underworld, but he was never, after Garfield's murder, able to hold public office. Banished from the national political arena, Conkling passed the last years of his life in relative obscurity. Walking alone along the streets of New York City in a blizzard, seven years after the President's assassination, Conkling fell among the snowdrifts; there, unaided, he remained until he had been fatally affected by exposure, and he died almost forgotten by the nation he had hoped to lead.

Guiteau's act was, of course, repudiated by the Stalwarts, just as Booth's crime was repudiated by the South, after the first reaction of spontaneous rejoicing Davis has himself recorded. In the public mind, however, the political nature of Guiteau's crime was recognized, and the inflammatory character of the attacks on Garfield by men who could not plead the excuse of being "mentally deranged" was held to have been the real cause of Guiteau's crime. In a contemporary issue of the authoritative *Cosmopolitan Magazine,* an article asserted, "When Guiteau was arrested, there was found on his person a copy of the *New York Herald* containing a severe arraignment of the President for his double-dealing with Conkling in the matter of New York appointments. The article was marked by Guiteau and it is supposed that he carried it about with him, reading it frequently and brooding over it, until his brain became inflamed with the murderous impulse." And the New York *Evening Telegraph,* on the day the crime had been committed, said that "to put a fact in plain language," Guiteau's act was a "natural outcome of the debased and debasing machine politics that this nation has suffered from ever since the war closed." *

While Guiteau was waiting for his trial, in prison, he had the occasion to reflect upon the rashness of his action. He could see now that it had been a miscalculation; that the Stalwarts on whom he had counted to approve his crime were not in a position to defend him. He was left now to his own resources, and when Garfield died, it was no longer mere imprisonment but the death sentence he was facing.

He could not deny that he was guilty of a crime which, like Jack Ruby, he had publicly committed. He would have to find another method of defense—and only one existed.

From the outset, as has been already stated, Guiteau had refused to face the fact that he had acted out of personal considerations, out of petty malice. He had sought a nobler

* Theodore Clarke Smith, *James Abram Garfield, Life and Letters.*

motive, trying to associate his grievance with those of all other office seekers in the Stalwart faction of the party. Since it now appeared that this was insufficient, he decided to seek justification for his action from an even higher source—from God Himself. To what extent expediency prompted this decision, no one now can say with certainty, but it suffices to observe that Guiteau's instinct for self-preservation and alleged religious feeling coincided with remarkable consistency throughout his trial. For there was only one way now to save his life, as Guiteau, with his legal background, knew quite well: to plead insanity, and furnish evidence supporting such a plea by acting like a madman.

In the medical profession there was, at this time, already stirring the first scientific protest against tendencies by the judicial system to condemn insane men to imprisonment when, doctors thought, they should instead be sent to mental institutions to be treated. Taking full advantage of America's preoccupation with this problem, Guiteau (guided by George Scoville, his brother-in-law, who was acting as his lawyer) managed to convert the courtroom, during the ten weeks in which his case was argued, into an amazing spectacle which seemed, at times, more like a lunatic asylum than a court of justice. He jumped up to interrupt opposing witnesses and counsel; gave long, incoherent speeches; said Jehovah had directed him to strike down Garfield, and concluded with the plea, "Let your verdict be that it was the Deity's act, not mine."

The judge who was presiding over this fantastic exhibition was severely criticized for letting Guiteau have full opportunity to demonstrate his madness, whether it was real or simulated. In response to this, *The Nation*, a contemporary magazine, declared, "The problem is, in short, whether, once a prisoner sets up insanity as a defense, it would not be passing on the question of his guilt or innocence to treat him in court as sane and responsible, and insist on his behaving as if his defense were a sham."

Guiteau was, therefore, given ample opportunity to build up a convincing case for his contention that he was a madman. After jurors had been told the stories of his previous eccentric acts and patiently submitted to a series of wild interruptions, the case was at last concluded and was studied by the jury, which deliberated for an hour and returned the verdict, "Sane and guilty." Guiteau was then executed.

The definitive, still-valid statement in respect to Guiteau and to others like him is the editorial appearing in *The Nation*, February 2, 1882. That magazine, among the most respected of its time, declared:

> The demonstrations of his insanity given by Guiteau were not successful. There is after all a certain method in madness. Even the crazy are crazy by certain rules, about which long experience has left little doubt, and Guiteau did not observe them. He did not conceal his acuteness or the rapidity and accuracy with which his judgment worked on things which concerned him deeply. The only proofs of his insanity he furnished were his violence and indifference to appearances, which are the marks of insanity which it is easiest to simulate—almost as easy, in fact, as to simulate the gait of a drunken man. The play of his mind in no other way indicated marked defectiveness. . . .
>
> If you are sane enough to live and do business in the world, and be treated in the ordinary relations of life as sane, and you plot or plan a crime beforehand, and in plotting and planning it, show that you know and fear its possible consequences, and have taken precautions against them, or made calculations to enable you to escape from them, you will be held responsible for the act and suffer the legal penalty. In other words, to be enabled to commit crime with impunity, it is not enough to be queer or eccentric, or cherish delusions about your own place in the world,

or exhibit incapacity for keeping your engagements. Your conduct for a long while before your crime must be such as to show that you were indifferent to the consequences of your acts. In other words, the doctrine of insanity *ad hoc,* as it were, or of sudden temporary insanity, lasting long enough to serve a particular unlawful purpose, has probably received the worst blow ever inflicted on it.

The Guiteau trial, unlike the previous proceedings following the Lincoln murder, was conducted in the modern era, under an interpretation of the law in which insanity was given a contemporary definition. It is the clear precedent which would have governed Lee H. Oswald's trial, had his lawyer pleaded the defendant was insane. It is perfectly apparent that, if such a genuine eccentric as Guiteau could be adjudged responsible for his acts under the judicial code of the United States, then Kennedy's presumed assassin was, to a far greater and more obvious degree, responsible for his crime also. As for Ruby, the preceding excerpt from *The Nation* admirably sums up reasons for rejecting "temporary insanity, lasting long enough to serve a particular unlawful purpose."

*　　　*　　　*

John Wilkes Booth was an assassin of the Right, and Charles J. Guiteau's Stalwarts, though more difficult to classify in that respect, may be considered to have been the right wing of their party. But since Lee H. Oswald, charged with Kennedy's assassination, has been called a crazy Leftist, it is fortunate that there exists a precedent for that charge, also. It will be illuminating to investigate, in this connection, the assassination of McKinley.

There has never been a President of the United States

whose foreign and domestic policy was more infuriating to the Left than the Republican, William McKinley, who was first elected in 1896 and re-elected four years later. For his contemporary counterpart, one is reminded of John Foster Dulles. President McKinley occupied the White House at the time when two events of a profound importance were occurring: the emergence of the U.S.A. as an imperialistic power with worldwide ambitions, and the ultimate consolidation of control by the big corporations and financial institutions over the American economy. It was under his administration that the war with Spain was sought, provoked and won, almost without resistance from the Spanish but with long and bloody opposition from some of the people in the former Spanish colonies which the United States invaded—indirectly occupying them after the war, as in Cuba, where the United States had imposed a long-term treaty which assured its economic domination of the island, or directly, as in the new colonies of Puerto Rico, Guam, Hawaii and the Philippines.

McKinley always had good moral reasons for his actions. In the war with Spain, the President refused to listen to his more extreme advisers, who declared the Cuban independence movement was a threat to the American investments on that island—sugar, iron and tobacco—and said U. S. troops should be dispatched to guard them without asking for the Spanish Government's permission. That was not McKinley's way of doing things, however. He preferred to wait for some external guidance and, while waiting, sent a battleship into the harbor of Havana, with instructions to protect the lives and property of the Americans in Cuba if there was a revolution. Three weeks after it arrived, it blew up, sinking to the bottom of the harbor. Spain, which had been desperately trying to avoid a war and knew itself to be defenseless, solemnly assured the world that it was not responsible for the explosion. Less than two months later, though, McKinley led an eager nation to declare war on the Spanish to avenge the battleship which, he charged, they had sunk. It was the cheapest war that any major power ever fought. No inch of soil, once captured, was surrendered; not one soldier in the U. S. troops was taken captive; and the casualties were confined almost entirely, on the U. S. side, to those who caught malaria or died from poisoned canned food profiteers had sold to the army.

As for annexation of the Philippines, McKinley said that God had told him that was what He wanted. In a talk before a group of clergymen, the President of the United States declared that he had asked God to reveal to him what he should do about those islands—and he said the answer came to him, miraculously, that it was the duty of America to send its troops there "and uplift and civilize and Christianize them," since these dark-skinned creatures were "our fellow men for whom Christ also died." The President informed the clergy that, when God had spoken to him this way, he called in the government's official map designer and directed him to mark the Philippines as U. S. property on all maps that he printed in the future. But the conquest of these islands did not prove as simple as the President had hoped. The deaths of natives fighting the United States to keep their independence have been estimated at about 600,000 in the Philippines alone; the U. S. Army lost 4,300. When American opponents of imperialism asked what rights their country planned to give the Filipino people, the reply McKinley offered was that it was "not a good time for the liberator to submit important questions concerning liberty and government to the liberated while they are engaged in shooting down their rescuers."

At home, McKinley's policies were those of multimillionaire Marcus A. Hanna, who had given him a large amount of money to repay a debt early in his political career and was, thereafter, his chief "adviser." Much had happened in America since Lincoln's time. The Civil War was fought for reasons more complex than those which customarily are given; from an economic standpoint, it was an alliance of the free Midwestern independent farmer with the Northern businessman and laborer against the big plantation owners of the South and those dependent on them. The Western agricultural economy was complemented by the Northern industry and commerce, and they traded chiefly with each other; but the South grew only food enough for its own needs, and its chief money crops were cotton and tobacco, which were then exported to the European market. The North, like any rising bourgeois nation, sought to shelter its new industries from European competition by protective tariffs, but the South, freely accepting a semi-colonial status, favored lower tariffs. Southerners were conscious of the fact that European countries had to sell goods in America to balance their commercial credits and permit them to continue buying Southern cotton and tobacco. Furthermore, the European manufactured goods, competing with the Northern products, would have lowered prices—and the South, in this field, had the interests of a consumer. The alliance of the Civil War days was already cracking in the time of Garfield, an ex-major general in Lincoln's army, who was backed by Western farmers in their struggle with the rich New Yorkers to control the party which had once elected Lincoln. In the years that followed Garfield's murder, the financial interests that had, in large part, backed the Stalwarts captured full control of the United States, and they were dominant in the political field also by the time McKinley came to be the candidate of the Republicans. The Sherman Anti-Trust Act, a law which had been intended to protect small business from the monopolies, was passed in 1890, but in 1896 McKinley was elected, and there were no prosecutions under his administration of the multimillion-dollar trusts established in defiance of this legislation, one of which was U. S. Steel, already at that time a billion-dollar corporation.

It was thus no ordinary President who came to Buffalo September 5, 1901, for the great exposition which had been erected in that city, celebrating the development of the United States as a world power in the past few years. McKinley rode up the Triumphal Causeway, made a speech, then toured the fairgrounds, had some coffee in the Puerto Rican Building, and that night watched a display of fireworks which included 22 enormous, fiery battleships traced in the sky. Next day, he came back for another look at the exhibits. In the afternoon, as was his habit, he had planned to shake hands with admirers in the crowd which came to see the fair. He had them lined up for him, and was walking past them, shaking first one hand and then another, when he came to someone who refused his hand and fired one shot into his breast, another through his abdomen. The President did not, however, die at once. McKinley, who was always well informed as to the will of the Creator, lingered for eight days, then told his wife, "It is God's way. His will, not ours, be done." His wife protested, "I want to go, too. I want to go, too," to which he answered, "We are all going. We are all going." A little after that, he went.

McKinley's murderer was knocked down, dragged across the hall and beaten, although he had offered no resistance. He turned out to be a workingman named Leon Czolgosz, twenty-eight years old, the son of Polish immigrants. When he was asked his motive, Czolgosz answered quietly, "I killed the President because he was the enemy of the good working people. I am not sorry for my crime."

To kill the President of the United States for "the good working people" was considered in America to be conclusive proof that Czolgosz was insane. When, under questioning, he said that he had once attended meetings held by socialists and anarchists, this first impression was confirmed. And when he told his lawyers that he knew that he would have to die, and would not help the court-appointed counsel to prepare his own defense, people were sure that he was crazy.

Anarchism, as a philosophical opinion—socialism, as an economic doctrine—to Americans like those who voted for McKinley, men who held such views were either mad conspirators or else conspiring madmen.

Little of the life of Czolgosz has been told, and what is known has been so colored by the views of his biographers that it is hard to reconstruct his character. His father was a common laborer who came to the United States from Poland. Leon Czolgosz was, however, born in the United States after his family's arrival. After he was old enough to work, he found employment in a Cleveland wire mill, was regarded as a conscientious and efficient worker, managing to hold his job when many other men were laid off during a depression. He remained there until 1898, when he fell sick and was obliged to find work which was less exhausting. While he was in Cleveland, he spent much time reading, and was thought by some of his associates to be "unsociable" and "quiet," but his conduct otherwise had been quite normal. The young workman took an interest in theoretical discussions on relationships of capital and labor, and attended lectures on that subject. Of the doctrines he examined, he was most attracted to the anarchist opinions.

After he was forced to search for lighter work, Leon decided to go home and help his father run a small farm which the family had purchased. He repaired the wagons and machinery, and tried to hunt for rabbits to help feed the family. His mother had been dead since he was twelve; his father had by now remarried, and there was continual dissension between Leon and his stepmother, who thought Leon spent too much time sleeping and reading, when he should have been out working. He eventually told his father that he couldn't stand her nagging any longer, and he asked the family to give him back the money he had lent them when they bought the farm. He took this money, and he went to live in Buffalo.

Leon Czolgosz, even while living on the farm, continued to be interested in the anarchist philosophy, and any act throughout the world attributed to anarchists attracted his attention. When King Humbert I of Italy was shot on July 29, 1900, by an anarchist who had until a short time previously been living in New Jersey, Czolgosz clipped the story from the paper and allegedly looked at it constantly. He tried on numerous occasions to join anarchist societies in Cleveland and Chicago, but there was so much repression of the anarchists at that time that they were distrustful of all strangers, fearing they were agents sent by the police to spy upon them. Czolgosz's ideas of anarchism were self-taught and ultraradical; they seemed to justify suspicion, and a publication of the U. S. anarchists called *Free Society* specifically warned its readers, in an issue which appeared five days before McKinley's murder, that Czolgosz was doubtless a provocateur and ought to be excluded from anarchist activity.

Notwithstanding this fact, it was felt that all the anarchists of the United States had been collectively responsible for the assassination of McKinley. Hundreds of them were tracked down, arrested and imprisoned. An attempt was made to prove that Czolgosz had accomplices among them, but no evidence was found that tended to confirm this general suspicion. All that could be definitely said—and here the charges were on firmer ground, and more deserving of attention—was that under certain circumstances, in specific times and places, anarchists of other nations had proposed and executed similar assassinations. And it is unquestionably true that Czolgosz' crime had been inspired entirely by his philosophical position—a position he, at least, defined as anarchist.

All three assassinations were, as we have seen, politically motivated, but the murder of McKinley is the only one in which no personal desire for glory or for vengeance was at any time revealed by the assassin. Booth leaped on the stage to make sure that the crowd would see the man who had the courage to shoot Lincoln from the back, and when he read newspaper stories of his crime, wrote in his diary: "I struck boldly, and not as the papers say. I walked with a firm step through thousands of his friends; was stopped, but pushed on. A colonel was at his side. I shouted Sic Semper before I fired. In jumping broke my leg. I passed all his pickets. Rode sixty miles that night, with the bone of my leg tearing the flesh at every jump. . . . I am abandoned, with the curse of Cain upon me, when, if the world knew my heart, that one blow would have made me great." Guiteau presented those who seized him with a letter which contained his own, somewhat exaggerated biography. But Czolgosz, when police asked him his name, said he was called Nieman—"Nobody" was his name. At no time did he indicate the feeling that he had been personally wronged. And in his jail cell, while his captors kept insisting that he should confess his hidden motive, Czolgosz told them only, "I thought it would be a good thing for the country."

Booth's co-plotters were allowed to plead their case for months, and so was Guiteau, but the trial of Czolgosz was rushed through to its conclusion in eight hours, and the jury found him guilty after a deliberation of precisely 34 minutes. He was then electrocuted, but the executioners did not permit his family to claim the corpse yet. First, they poured the contents of a large container of carbolic acid over his dead body, as it lay within the coffin. This last gesture—punishing the corpse of the "insane" assassin—was, McKinley backers thought, the work of sane men.

The assassination of McKinley merely served to transfer power to a man who—although less subservient to the monopolies at home—was, in his foreign policy, still more imperialistic. For McKinley was not, in himself, the driving force behind America's expansionist ambitions; he was just their spokesman. There were many others, like the Senator from Indiana, Beveridge, who said, "God has made us the master organizers of the world to establish system where chaos reigns. . . . He has marked the American people as His chosen nation to finally lead in the regeneration of the world. This is the divine mission of America." And even such a sober man as William Allen White, America's most famous editor and White House counselor, declared, "It is the Anglo-Saxon's manifest destiny to go forth as a world conqueror." But the consequence of the McKinley assassination was to elevate into the White House the supreme imperialist of them all, Theodore Roosevelt, for whom the McKinley policies were held to be too cautious. Once, impatient with delays in launching the attack on Cuba, he had said that President McKinley, who was searching for some moral justification for the war, "had no more backbone than a chocolate eclair." *

Unlike the first two assassinations, the McKinley murder did not reverse political positions taken under the preceding administration; it confirmed them in the course in which they were already heading. One may, therefore, question the efficacity of isolated acts of terror, even from the point of view of those who plan them and perform them. But the advocacy of such acts is an intrinsic part of a worldwide, historic revolutionary movement—or, at least, that part of it which follows Bakunin. It would be naïve to argue that an ideology which has attracted millions of adherents cannot be adopted by a man who is not crazy.

* Margaret Leech, *In the Days of McKinley.*

No convincing, independent proof of Czolgosz' madness ever has been offered. Nor did any court find him insane. The whole assumption rests upon the specious argument that the adherence to a certain ideology is *ipso facto* evidence of madness. Yet no statement ever was attributed to Czolgosz which can match in simple madness the assertion made by Roosevelt, just before hostilities began in Cuba, that, because so many people wanted peace, there ought to be a war: "The clamor of the peace faction has convinced me that this country needs a war. . . . I rather hope the fight will come soon."

*   *   *

With this historical review of previous assassinations, we are now in a position to evaluate the statement which has been repeated in the magazines and journals on which most Americans depend for facts on which to form their judgment—that all Presidents of the United States to date who fell by an assassin's bullet were the victims of deranged men who had no accomplices and no political objective.

This was not the first official explanation, it must be restated. At the outset, it was held that Oswald was an agent of the Communist world revolutionary movement, and that Ruby had been an indignant patriot who took the law into his hands in order to avenge the martyred leader and his brave young widow. It was only *after* Ruby's motives had been almost universally suspected that another version of the crime was substituted: Oswald was a solitary madman; so was Ruby; and they did not know each other. And, since no specific proof that Oswald was a madman could be offered, the new theory rested solely on continual assertions that, historically, this had been the *only* explanation

66

for the previous attacks, that a political assassination had not ever happened in the U.S.A.

I take as an example of this point of view the article in *Time*, November 29, 1963, a week after the crime in Dallas:

> Assassination has never been an instrument of politics in the U.S.: no plot to seize power, no palace intrigue, has ever cost an American President his life. The three assassins whose bullets killed Presidents Lincoln, Garfield and McKinley were lonely psychopaths, adrift from reason in a morbid fascination with the place history gives those who reverse its orderly progress. Each sought an hour of mad glory—and each died convinced that history would understand.

Time says Booth was just a "lonely psychopath" without political objectives. That this statement is historically false needs scarcely any further demonstration. It is also a distortion of the character of the assassin, for in Richmond and in other Southern cities where he acted, Booth had lived a life which certainly cannot be properly described as "lonely." He had been the pampered darling of aristocrats and politicians, and his prejudices were not his alone. They were the feelings of the social group in which he moved, whose confidences he enjoyed; he shared their dinners and, whenever opportunities arose, he shared their wives and daughters. One of these, whose father was a Senator, had been so indiscreet, in the first breathless flush of her seduction, as to confirm in writing her relationship with the young, handsome actor. She had written a quotation from a poem under some phrase Booth had written, and had signed the note "in John's room." Booth, of course, had boasted later over this young lady's indiscretion, and the incident created something of a scandal. In discussing it among his friends, Booth doubtless tended to exaggerate the depth and number of the thrusts and parries, as he later did when he related how he had to fight his way past "thousands" of the President's armed guards to fire a shot into the brain of Lincoln. Not all braggarts are insane, however. Booth moved in what would be called today the "cocktail set," of which he was a popular young member. The lesser members of the plot obeyed him for this very reason. They considered him a "gentleman" and knew that he had the respect and aid of influential friends.

One unfamiliar with the history of the United States—and most Americans, unfortunately, fall into this category—would not guess that Booth's co-plotters went on trial. *Time* does not mention the court proceedings. And in telling of the circumstances of the Garfield murder, *Time*'s account is based entirely on the very evidence the court rejected—all the stories Guiteau's lawyer introduced in an attempt to prove his client was a madman and thus win his freedom. Here again, *Time* says there was no "element of politics" in the assassination, no attempt to transfer power from one faction to another—this despite the fact that Guiteau shouted, as he fired, "I am a Stalwart, and Arthur is President now!" In fact, *Time* manages to give a summary of this case without any mention of the Stalwarts. So profoundly did the people of that epoch feel Guiteau's act to have been political, however, that the President who took his place was forced to put an end to the worst evils of the system of political appointments which, it was agreed, provoked the murder—and to break with Roscoe Conkling and the Stalwart faction of the party, with which he had always been associated. None of these facts appear in *Time*'s account.

On the other hand, the thesis that U. S. assassinations never are political in nature seems to undergo a certain transformation when *Time* starts discussing Czolgosz and McKinley. *Time* says Czolgosz was an anarchist in the first sentence. In the second sentence, just to make sure that the reader knows the murderer's political affiliation, the word "anarchist" is then repeated. It appears in the third sentence, also. And the fact that anarchists throughout the country who did not know Czolgosz or have any contact with him were arrested after the assassination shows the government considered that his crime was not committed by a "lonely psychopath" but by a member of a revolutionary party, membership in which was, from that time, forbidden.

Yet, despite this, *Time* at last concludes, "All three killers were very likely insane."

This fits in neatly with the F.B.I.'s conclusion in regard to Oswald's motives, summarized in *The New York Times* of January 26, 1964, as follows: "He had no known motive. . . . The only explanation now offered is that Oswald was insane."

What does the F.B.I. mean when it employs the word "insane"?

Does it refer to any definition that would be accepted by a doctor?

There are now, in the United States, more than 600,000 persons classified by medical examination as sufficiently deranged in mind to need continuous attention in a mental institution. Since these people are already in confinement they may be excluded from suspicion. During each twelve months, a quarter of a million other citizens of the United States develop mental illness so acute that it requires hospital treatment, while a slightly smaller number are released provisionally, on the judgment of physicians that they are not psychopathic. Thus, the number of incipient psychotic or potentially regressive cases who remain at liberty does not, at any given time, exceed 500,000. Any murder by a member of this group might be provisionally diagnosed as having been committed by a person who did not have any reasonable motive, but was simply acting as the consequence of mental illness. There has been no evidence of any act committed by Lee Harvey Oswald prior to the President's assassination or thereafter which affords the slightest reason to assign him to this category.

Victims of psychoses who remain at liberty are, for the most part, harmless. Any news reporter who has manned the City Desk at night has met them by the dozens and, in general, they are considerably more benevolent toward humanity than sane men. Most of them have projects that they want to give to mankind, freely. Presidents a hundred years ago used to be bothered, now and then, by the necessity of listening to their entreaties; modern Presidents are busier and have more bureaucrats to guard them. Once, when Hayes was President, an incident of this type did take place. The President had asked his secretary whether there were any more appointments. "No," the secretary answered, "but there are some people here who say that they would like to see you." Hayes demanded wearily how many of them were still waiting. "Only two," the secretary told him, "and there's no use bothering with one of them. He's absolutely crazy." "All right," Hayes responded with a sigh. "Send in the sane one." In a little while, the President sent an impatient summons. "Is this fellow meant to be the sane one?" he inquired discreetly. Glancing at the man who had been talking to the President, the secretary nodded. "Well, he introduced himself as the World Emperor," said Hayes. "Send in the one who's crazy."

It must be assumed, if there is any merit in the thesis that the murderer of Kennedy was "crazy," that he was a paranoid who thought that he was being personally persecuted; that, like Guiteau, he had nursed some private grievance until it had come to be obsessive, and he felt the only way in which he could avenge the wrong that had been done him was to fire the murder weapon. But since Oswald is the only suspect who has been officially accused, acceptance of this thesis would imply that Kennedy was not the target—that the shots were fired, instead, at Texas Governor John Connally. There has not ever been the slightest indication of a private injury which Oswald felt that he had suffered at the hands of Kennedy himself. Police at Dallas charged, however, that Lee Oswald once had sent a letter threatening the life of Connally, who had been Secretary of the Navy in September, 1959, when Oswald was released from active duty at his own request in order to support his mother. When he subsequently tried to swear allegiance to the Soviet Union, he was given a discharge from the Marine reserves as "undesirable," as might have been expected. The reports first issued were that Oswald had thereafter menaced Connally, feeling his military service had been honorable—as, indeed, it had—and that his subsequent political decision had no relevance to the performance of his duty while he was in uniform. But when the contents of the letter Oswald wrote in early 1962 to Connally were known, the "threats of violence" turned out to be no more specific than the phrase, "I shall employ all means to right this gross mistake or injustice to a bona fide U. S. citizen and ex-serviceman"—hardly the basis for belief that he was planning to assassinate him. A deranged man who was brooding over his rejection by his former military service would have made some effort, on returning to the United States, to rejoin it; but there is no record that he ever tried to do so. Connally, moreover, played no role in the Marines' decision; he replied to Oswald's letter that the matter was no longer in his jurisdiction, and that it had been referred to his successor. Any feeling of hostility that Oswald might have had would thus, presumably, have been diverted to the man who ultimately had rejected his request, or to the officer who signed his discharge in the first place. If, by some insane illogic, Connally had been in fact the target, is it likely that the murderer would choose the day when Kennedy was riding in the car beside him, with a huge armed escort; or that, firing three shots, he would hit the wrong man twice?

No personal affront had been inflicted on Lee Oswald by the President himself, or by the office that he represented. The United States had given him the money that he asked for, to return from Russia and to bring his wife and family back with him; it had given him a passport to go back there, if it pleased him; nothing Oswald had requested of the government had been denied him. But if he were paranoid and had some secret grievance, how would he have acted *after* the assassination? Such a murderer would certainly have made no effort to escape. If he believed himself to be the victim of some kind of persecution which the President, or those responsible to him, was hiding, he would want to tell the world about it. He would make no effort to conceal the reasons for his act. An audience would be precisely what he had been seeking. He would hope that people, after they had heard his story, would agree that he had been unjustly treated. It is hardly likely that a murderer of this sort, in the exaltation of his long-awaited vengeance, would be governed by considerations of self-preservation, that he would immediately plead "Not Guilty," like an income tax evader. Nor could such a murderer withstand two days of constant questioning without betraying his psychotic nature. An assassination by a madman—one who would be so regarded by a doctor—may thus be excluded as an explanation of the crime in Dallas. It could not have been conceived and executed by a person permanently stricken with a mental illness.

Does the F.B.I. imply, however, that the murderer was *temporarily* "insane"? Such an assassin would have had some reason for the murder but the crime would, under this interpretation, not have been premeditated. Pleas of "temporary" madness have, in the United States in recent years, become so common that misuse of this sometimes-legitimate defense is now a scandal. Many lawyers use it automatically when their client's guilt is so apparent, as in the Jack Ruby case, that it is useless to deny the fact. It then becomes a shield for that insanity "ad hoc" of which *The Nation* warned in 1882, which lasts only so long as may be necessary to accomplish "a particular unlawful purpose," and thereafter guarantees immunity from prosecution, or results in a substantially diminished penalty. A large proportion of all murders are, in fact, committed during a brief period in which the murderer's behavior is abnormal due to some strong passion, jealousy or sudden indignation, under influence of drugs or in a drunken frenzy. Acts committed at such moments are not planned and may, a short time later, be regretted. But assassination is no ordinary crime, and, more than any other type of murder, an assassination of the President requires premeditation, since the President at all times is surrounded by trained men whose only function is to guard him—men who have at their disposal all the latest means of transportation and communication. It requires a careful plan for an assassin to outwit them, and it takes considerable patience. Booth and his assistants had been searching for a way to strike at Lincoln for a year. Guiteau and Czolgosz made long, careful preparations. And whoever killed the President in Dallas could not possibly have acted from a sudden impulse. All the evidence points to a thorough, scientific planning of the crime. Nor does it seem conceivable that an assassin temporarily deranged by sudden passion could, immediately after, at the culmination of his frenzy, stand and drink a Coca-Cola. Certainly the President was not the victim of a crime of sudden passion.

Now, if the assassin's madness was not either permanent or temporary, one is forced to the conclusion that it was of no duration—that the murderer was not insane, not even

73

for a moment. Nor, indeed, was he regarded as psychotic by authorities in Dallas—not so long as he was living. If the suspect had been brought before a judge and jury, any prosecution lawyer would have been obliged to show that the defendant knew what he was doing—that the crime had been premeditated. So the prosecution would have been required to prove a motive.

If Lee Harvey Oswald were alive today—if he had not been murdered in Police Headquarters—no one would be calling him insane except, perhaps, his own defense attorney. That is the ironic part about it. The same people who are now insisting he was crazy would have been the first, if he were living, to demand that he be punished as a sane man for premeditated murder. For the only time a prosecutor says that the defendant was insane is when he's trying to convict a dead man. Such convictions can be useful only when they shield the living.

And when an investigating agency declares that it can find no motive for the President's assassination but the murderer's insanity, it does not mean that no such motive can be found. It means, perhaps, that the investigation was a failure.

*   *   *

We have earned the right, now, to demand of any explanation of the President's assassination that it be consistent. We have earned the right to test its logic, to make it believable in terms of human nature. The contention that the flaws in an hypothesis can be explained by blandly stating that the individual responsible for the assassination was himself irrational can be rejected.

We have made a long digression—one the author of this

book would not have chosen, were it not that the official or quasi-official explanation of insanity forced us to do so. We have made a long digression—possibly somebody with an interest in this case wanted us to do that. But we have returned now to the point where we began it.

Why would any Communist or person of pro-Communist opinions act as though he were an anti-Communist? This was the question we had been asking. For the anti-Communist effect of the announcement of the murderer's alleged political affiliation was, as anyone could easily have forecast, overwhelming, and to the extent that the original hypothesis is still believed, remains so. This effect was obvious from the beginning to the right-wing press, and the Hearst papers instantly proclaimed, "As now is clear the assassination was committed by a Communist fanatic unaware of the depth of evil to which such dogma could lead him. *In so doing he served the Communist cause its worst setback in the 46 years since its baneful inception.*" *

Why would any Leftist hand his enemies this weapon? we demanded. And the answer which was tentatively given was that Oswald, the presumed assassin, must have been a *crazy* Marxist, not an ordinary, sane one. We can now definitely state that he was *not* insane by any definition, medical or legal.

And the Communists were not collectively insane enough to sponsor such a project. We have been assured by no less an authority on their activities than F.B.I. Director Hoover that there is no evidence of any Communist connection with the Oswald plot. And it is manifest that they obtained no benefit from it, but on the contrary it threatened to provoke an inquisition which would liquidate the left-wing movement in the U.S.A., discredit Khrushchev and perhaps inspire a vengeful nation to invade the

* Baltimore *News-Post*, November 23, 1963 (italics added).

75

Cubans. It is the unchanged position of the President's Commission, also, that no outside help from any source was given, or could possibly have been received, by Oswald. Thus the possibility of any Communist conspiracy is totally excluded.

Is it possible, however, that a sane but solitary Marxist, an embittered "man without a country," acted on his own initiative for what he thought, sincerely though mistakenly, would serve some Communist objective?

Although this hypothesis may seem more plausible than either of the first two, it is likewise false, and for two reasons. Either of these reasons is conclusive:

First, that Lee H. Oswald could not possibly have been alone; and

Second, that he could not possibly have been a Leftist.

*   *   *

Some preliminary comments are in order, prior to detailed analysis of the official explanation of this crime.

The thesis which will be described hereafter as "official" will be that which law-enforcement officers in Dallas or in Washington have told the nation, and which ultimately was confirmed by publication of the findings of the President's Commission. Where these findings differ from original official statements, an attempt is made to trace their evolution.

Any inquiry as grave in its potential consequences as the Kennedy investigation normally would be expected to have started with a great variety of theories, which would each have been explored by the investigating agencies and then discarded as new evidence was gathered which appeared to contradict it.

What distinguishes this case from the accepted pattern of police investigation of a murder in which there was neither a confession nor a witness able to identify the killer is the fact that the procedure has been the exact reverse. That is to say, investigators have adhered to one hypothesis from the beginning—that the murderer had no accomplice—and it is the supporting evidence, including facts so vital as the weapon, the trajectory of bullets and the number and the nature of the wounds which keeps continually changing to conform to that hypothesis.

Citizens of the United States, observing that investigators have produced at least four reinterpretations of the way the shots were fired—each one irreconcilable with all the others—and that they have nonetheless deduced from this divergent evidence the same, unvarying conclusion, may be pardoned if they start to wonder whether the machinery of the investigation does not have some built-in flaw that predisposes it in one direction.

If, as a statistician, I were solving problems with the aid of a machine and I discovered that, however the components of my problem altered, the machine would always give me the same answer, I should be inclined to think that the machine was broken.

*   *   *

Before we start to analyze the crime, let me first set the scene, as you yourself would see it were you to go down to Dallas and retrace the path that John F. Kennedy was taking on November 22nd.

You have landed first at an efficient, modern airport called Love Field, gone past a statue of a Texas Ranger which was recently erected to bear tribute to the efficacy of police in Texas with a motto indicating that it takes only one Ranger to suppress a riot. Then, pursuing the parade route, you have passed the famed department store and the tall office buildings for which Dallas now is noted and have come at last down Main Street to the fateful corner, Main and Houston. Within a few hundred yards of this spot, most of the events connected with the Kennedy assassination took place. You have just gone past the city jail where Oswald was shot down by Ruby, and the courthouse where Jack Ruby was himself condemned. The office buildings are behind you now. Before you is a small park, Dealey Plaza, formed by the convergence of three streets in a triangle—Main Street, on which you are riding, and the streets on either side of it, Commerce and Elm, which have been running parallel to Main Street but which now descend abruptly and pass side by side together, separated only by a concrete strip, beneath a railway trestle.

If you turned left into Houston Street, the first building between you and the railroad tracks would be a post office. Next would come a warehouse in which bags of mail are loaded and unloaded from the trains, and after that is Union Station with its waiting rooms for railway passengers. Beyond this building there is nothing but the warehouse of Railway Express, after which Houston Street becomes a viaduct closed to pedestrians and there are no more buildings. Opposite the railroad terminal on Houston Street there is a park, and the whole area between the park and viaduct is occupied by one large building, where Jack Ruby states he was located when the President was shot. It is the Dallas *Morning News*.

But if, instead of turning to the left toward the railway station, you now made a right turn at the intersection of Main Street and Houston, following the President's parade route, you would travel one short block and then—since Houston comes to a dead end a half block farther—make a sharp turn leftward into Elm Street and once more be headed down beneath the railroad tracks. As you descended Elm Street, there would not be anything now on your left except the wide expanse of Dealey Plaza; on your right, there would be only one more office building, a school book depository on the corner. Elm Street, after turning to the left in order to converge with Main Street, then veers gradually to the right in order to reduce the angle at which the converging traffic will be forced to turn when Elm Street, Main and Commerce meet and all run parallel beneath the railroad tracks together. As you come toward these tracks, the bridge that bears them is, of course, above you, although at the intersection of Elm Street and Houston you were at the level of the tracks. The short block you have traveled has thus taken you on a downgrade, and on a slow arc to the right after a sharp turn leftward. The railroad bridge now looms before you and on either side, as you approach it, there are steep grass slopes that lead up from the sidewalk to the railway tracks, which mark the end of downtown Dallas.

Somewhere along the journey you have taken, Kennedy was shot. Let us now analyze the manner in which this was done, according to official explanations.

THE OFFICIAL THESIS: That the probable itinerary of the President's parade route during his projected trip to Dallas was known to Lee Harvey Oswald when he asked for, and obtained, work at the Texas School Book Depository; that he chose the job because he knew the building in which he would work contained an ideal sniper's nest; and that he knew that the President would pass directly underneath the sixth-floor window where he would be waiting with his rifle.

This charge, confidently made in the beginning, was thereafter steadily downgraded by investigators of the crime, as it became apparent that only a handful of insiders charged with organizing Kennedy's reception could have known the path the presidential motorcade would take as early as October 15th, when Lee Oswald went to work in the school book depository. All that had been settled at that time was that the President was planning soon to come to Dallas.

Yet District Attorney Henry Wade announced November 24th that the police had found in Oswald's rented room what Wade described as one of the most damning elements in the official case against him—evidence that proved the crime had been premeditated from the time that Oswald went to work on Elm Street. It was said to be a map on which a number of alternative locations for the murder had been marked by Oswald. One of these—the book depository —was not only marked, but had a line beside it which, Wade said, traced out the planned trajectory of the projected bullets.

Wade acknowledged that he had not seen the map himself, but based his charges on reports he had received from the police. When federal investigators later analyzed the map, however, they concluded that the first, sensational interpretation of its use had been romanticized, to put it mildly. Oswald, who was not a native and was unfamiliar with the streets of Dallas, had been given it to help him to report to his new job.

Nor did Lee Oswald know, when he applied for work, that he would be assigned to the warehouse on Elm Street, since the company that hired him operates another building at a different location. There was at that time "no definite opening" in either office, according to Roy S. Truly, who said later that he gave Oswald the job because he thought he was an ex-serviceman who needed work. He could, accordingly, have made a place for him in either building; Oswald could not have foreseen where his new job would be located.

The possibility that Oswald, at that time, could have been interested in the Elm Street warehouse as a prospective sniper's nest is, furthermore, excluded by the fact that, if original plans had not been subsequently altered, Kennedy would not have passed through downtown Dallas but would have been driven from the airport directly to his luncheon engagement at the Trade Mart. The route taken is by no means the direct one. It involves a long detour. A number of alternative sites for the President's reception was proposed, debated and rejected; each one would have meant a different parade route from the one eventually chosen; and it is one of the saddest ironies of the assassination that if the request of Dallas Negro leaders had been heeded, Kennedy would have passed through the Negro section, far from the impending ambush. It was not until November 13th that police were sure enough of the reception plans to start to map the President's parade route. No one but the most influential of the Dallas civic leaders could have said with any certainty, until that time, where it would go.

THE OFFICIAL THESIS: That the shots fired at the presidential car all came from one man standing at the southeast corner window on the sixth floor of the book depository.

The eyewitness testimony tended, from the outset, to negate this thesis. The consensus of policemen and civilians present was that the first shot had come from the direction of the bridge which spans the triple underpass toward which Kennedy was heading; that the bullets came, thereafter, from the opposite direction; that the first shot "sounded different" from all the others; that two of the shots "came very close together." This is the description of an ambush, in which two or more men catch their victim in a crossfire, making it more difficult for their intended target to evade them, and eventually covering their own retreat.

The first shot, of course, was the most difficult to designate, since no one had expected it, while after that it was a relatively easy matter to determine the direction from which subsequent shots were coming.

Probably the witnesses best qualified to testify to the direction from which the first shot was fired were those who had been trained by their profession to detect and recognize the source of gunfire, and whose job it was that day to be on the alert at all times for an incident of that sort. This would, notably, include the driver of the presidential car and the policeman mounted on the nearest motorcycle, B. W. Hargis. Hargis told the Dallas *Times Herald,* "About halfway down between Houston and the underpass, I heard the first shot. It sounded like a real loud firecracker." It was Hargis' responsibility, as one charged with protection of the President, to rush in the direction of the danger, and accordingly he darted forward, feeling the shot "might have come from the trestle." The responsibility of Kennedy's chauffeur was the reverse; he was instructed, naturally, to drive in the opposite direction from the source of danger. It is, thus, of great significance to note that he did not speed up at once, as he would certainly have done if he had thought the shot had come from the school book depository, which was now behind him. On the contrary, during the first few seconds after all the passengers began to cry out that the President was wounded, the chauffeur appeared to hesitate as though he felt that he was heading into greater danger. Nerin E. Gun, author of *The Red Roses of Dallas,* described it this way after viewing photographs: "The car's chauffeur was looking straight ahead, toward the bridge, trying to find out what had caused this sound." It was not until the shots could definitely be located in the rear that he stepped down on the accelerator—not, in short, until the second or the third shot. The time which elapsed is far more than can be attributed to a slow reflex.

The official statement of Policeman Seymour Weitzman, who is credited with having found the murder weapon in the book depository, likewise indicates a disbelief that all the shots had come from that direction. The report he signed November 23rd declares that he was stationed at the intersection of Main Street and Houston when he heard the first shot. "I ran northwest in the direction of the shots," he stated, "but then someone shouted, 'Go to the Old Texas Building.' " To a person at Main Street and Houston, "northwest" would have been located in the general direction of that portion of the bridge which passes over Elm Street, and this officer did not go back toward the book depository (also known as the Old Texas Building) on the basis of his own judgment but because he was directed by a superior officer to do so.

The officer who was convinced from the beginning that the shots had all come from the book depository was Police Chief Jesse Curry, who was leading the parade in a car just before the one in which the President was riding. "Moments after the fatal shot was fired . . . Chief Curry said, he radioed instructions that the Texas School Book Depository Building be surrounded and searched," *The New York Times* reported November 24th. "The chief was riding in a car 40 feet ahead of the limousine carrying Mr. and Mrs. Kennedy. . . . Chief Curry said he could tell from the sound of the three shots that they had come from the book company's building."

Chief Curry was almost beneath the railway bridge when the first shot was fired. But Roy S. Truly, Oswald's boss, was standing at the entrance of the book depository, and he told reporters that he had not thought the shots were coming from the sixth-floor window under which he had been standing when the firing started. In a conversation with a private investigator, Truly stated, "Most of the people on the sidewalk at the time thought the shots had come from between the overpass and knoll," but he asserted that police have now convinced him that he must have been mistaken. O. V. Campbell, the vice-president of Truly's firm, who had been standing near the entrance to the building, had the same reaction. He was quoted as declaring that he actually ran in the direction of the underpass in an attempt to spot the sniper.

Mary E. Woodward, a reporter for the Dallas *Morning News*, was standing on the grassy slope between the overpass—located on her right—and the book depository, on her left. She wrote, in her eyewitness story, that the President had turned in her direction just before the first shot hit him. "After acknowledging our cheering, he faced forward again and suddenly there was a horrible, ear-shattering noise coming from behind us and a little to the right," i.e., from the direction of the railway bridge.

Charles Drehm, who had been standing on the Elm Street pavement a few feet from the President when the first shot rang out, said he thought that it came, not from the rear, but from "in front of" Kennedy. He added that the President slumped backward for a moment; he did not at once slump forward, as this witness felt he would have done if the first bullet had struck him from the rear. The sound of the first shot, he stated, tended to confirm his feeling that it came from somewhere on or near the bridge.

Is there any evidence to show that there was actually someone on the railway bridge at the exact time that the shots were fired? Police at first denied this. By the time the President's Commission published its report, however, they admitted there were 13 people scattered over the long bridge across Elm, Main and Commerce streets, and that policemen "guarding" this bridge had allowed them to remain there because they identified themselves as railroad workers. Why a railroad worker was presumed to be less likely to provoke an incident than anybody else, at that time, is not stated by the President's Commission. No one, prior to release of the report of the Commission, had reported seeing any of these railroad workers on the bridge at that time. That must be regarded as surprising since, if they were there, they had the best eyewitness view of the whole scene of anyone who witnessed the assassination. Other witnesses besieged reporters, offering to tell what happened—some of them for money—but the railroad workers on the bridge apparently were timid, self-effacing Texans who preferred to keep their presence there a secret.

There is proof, however, that two people who did *not* appear to have been railroad workers—one of them a woman—were seen on the bridge.

"Reporters following the President," according to George Carter in the Dallas *Times Herald* of November 22nd, "said a man and woman were seen scrambling on a walk over the underpass." The first radio reports which followed the assassination said the fleeing couple had been chased by a policeman on a motorcycle, who had raced up an embankment after them, but his pursuit presumably was thwarted by a wire fence which protects a parking lot behind which they were heading.

Confirmation of the view of these eyewitnesses and others that the shots had come from two directions was supplied when surgeons who had seen the President as he was brought into Parkland Memorial Hospital in Dallas, and who subsequently operated on him, told reporters that the first shot struck the President directly from the front, the last one at an angle from the rear. They were aware at the time that they made this statement that Police Chief Jesse Curry had asserted that all shots had come from the school book depository, in the rear. Dr. Robert R. Shaw,

85

the director of the hospital's department of thoracic surgery, admitted that he was "a little baffled" to discover that one bullet had entered the front of the President's body, despite police reports. But the Dallas surgeons were unanimous on this point. *The New York Times* reported on November 27th, "Dr. Kemp Clark, who pronounced Mr. Kennedy dead, said one struck him at about the necktie knot. 'It ranged downward in his chest and did not exit,' the surgeon said." The President's second injury was called by Dr. Clark a "tangential wound" caused by a bullet that struck "the right side of his head."

Thus, initially, there was a strong presumption that the crime had been committed by at least two persons. *This, it should be noted, was the first opinion of District Attorney Henry Wade himself.* The Dallas *Morning News* of November 23rd declared, "Wade said preliminary reports indicated more than one person was involved in the shooting," and they quoted him as saying, "The electric chair is too good for the killers."

Some time after this spontaneous interpretation of the first reports that reached him, Henry Wade revised his views completely, and adopted the position of Police Chief Curry that the crime was carried out by one man.

It appears this change was influenced, and very possibly determined, by the intervention of authorities in Washington. The information given by the agencies on which he was relying to the new President of the United States, Lyndon B. Johnson, in the first few hours after he took office seems to have led him to the conclusion that, since Oswald had just come back from the Soviet Union, any talk of a conspiracy with one or more accomplices would seriously menace U. S.-Soviet relations and conceivably might jeopardize world peace. The full weight of the United States Government's discreet but urgent intervention based on this assumption (later felt, like many other recent intel-

86

ligence reports on which our government has acted, to have been without foundation) seems to have been aimed at curbing the attempt of right-wing elements in Dallas, using evidence that tended to show Oswald had accomplices, to spread reports of a Moscow-directed plot.

This was the origin of that uneasy pact, which has persisted to this day, between a liberal Administration in Washington and the municipal authorities in the Republican stronghold of Dallas, in which each side undertook, by gentleman's agreement, to deny existence of a plot which might reflect discredit on the other.

The position of Police Chief Curry that the shots all came from the school book depository corresponded with what Washington regarded as the interests of national security. Curry's position was, thereafter, that of Henry Wade, who said November 23rd there was no doubt the crime had been committed by a single man without accomplices from any group, either of the left or the right wing.

There was one apparent flaw in Curry's theory: It was difficult to reconcile the medical reports that one shot had been fired from someone facing the assassination victim with the homicide report, which stated that the car had been receding from the book depository when the murderer had opened fire. The first official version of the shooting was, therefore, withdrawn. A second version followed. The police declared the car had not yet turned the corner when the firing started. Oswald had fired one shot from the corner window as the car approached him, and continued firing as the car receded. The police declared that they had witnesses who were prepared to swear this was the way it happened—and no doubt they did.

The press then dutifully printed this new, contradictory official explanation. It was summarized as follows in the New York *Herald Tribune* of November 27th: "On the basis of accumulated data, investigators have concluded that the first shot, fired as the presidential car was approaching, struck the President in the neck just above the knot of his necktie, then ranged downward into his body."

This second explanation proved untenable, however. By an accident, an amateur photographer had made a motion picture of the whole assassination. Prints from his film appeared in *Life* November 29th, and made it possible to calculate with great precision the exact location of the presidential car each time the President was struck, and the interval between the shots. The car had made its left turn at the corner where the book depository was located and had continued for approximately 50 yards toward the railroad bridge before the first shot was fired. The President had been facing the front of the car when he was struck; he continued to face in this direction after he was shot; he could not, therefore, have been wounded in the front by any marksman shooting from the book depository, which was now behind him.

For two weeks, federal investigators wrestled with this difficult dilemma. They rehearsed the crime, attempting to discover some way to resolve the problem. Re-enactments were still taking place as late as December 5th, according to *The New York Times* of the following date, to answer "how the President could have received a bullet in the front of the throat from a rifle in the Texas School Book Depository Building after his car had passed the building and was turning a gentle curve away from it."

For the second time, the facts appeared to contradict the thesis that the shots were fired from one direction. The investigators did not revise their thesis. There was a new re-evaluation of the facts. The second version of the shooting was withdrawn. A third one followed. This time, the position of the car when the first shot was fired and the location of the wound were both reversed. The third official version was that all the shots—and therefore all the wounds—were in the rear. The throat wound was, according to the new interpretation, not caused by a bullet's entry but by exit of a bullet fragment. The new sequence was described as follows: Bullet One hit Kennedy on his right shoulder, a few inches underneath the collar. It did not cause any damage to the throat at all; it would not have been fatal. After a small penetration, it lodged in the victim's shoulder. Bullet Two, as had been previously thought, struck Connally. The fatal bullet was the third one which, as Dallas surgeons had asserted, penetrated the skull of the victim. Then, however, contrary to their belief, a bullet sliver was deflected and passed out the throat. The chest wound was presumably caused by another sliver of this shattered bullet.

The authority for this sweeping revision of the very detailed surgical report issued in Parkland Memorial Hospital, which had been widely publicized and never previously challenged, was said to have been the autopsy findings, which had been available to the investigators the whole time they had been trying to explain why Kennedy was facing the first shot that hit him. The autopsy was conducted late November 22nd at Bethesda Naval Hospital near Washington. A "high White House source" had said the next day that the doctors at Bethesda had removed a bullet from the chest of the dead President. This coincided with the story that had been released in Dallas. The autopsy had, accordingly, not yet been classified as secret and, if it revealed the Dallas surgeons to have been, in some respects, in error, it is not clear why this fact was not at once made public.

Were the Dallas doctors wrong, however? The new version of the wounds appeared to solve one problem, but created others. How, for instance, could the whole hospital staff at Parkland have failed to observe the back wound? Washington explained that there had been no nurse or doctor, from the time the President was brought in until he was carried out, who had an opportunity to see it, since he had been lying on his back. They got two surgeons to confirm this: Dr. Malcolm Perry, who performed the operation, and Dr. Robert N. McClelland, who assisted in the desperate attempt to restore the patient's breathing. Both agreed, after a visit by the federal investigators, that they had been too busy with more vital tasks to have observed the back wound, if there was one.

It may plausibly be argued that a relatively minor wound could pass unnoticed, as a man lay dying on the operating table. Is it in the region of belief, however, that the man who signed the death certificate, knowing the victim was the President of the United States and that he had been murdered, did not think it was important to ascertain the location and the number of external wounds—that he confined his attention to the portion of the dead man's body which happened to be turned in his direction? The distinguished surgeon who performed this function did not associate himself with the public statement of the first two doctors, which was widely hailed as a "retraction."

One can readily appreciate the difficult position in which Drs. Perry and McClelland had been placed. They did not wish to contradict the findings of their colleagues in Bethesda. In addition to the normal ethics of the medical profession, they were conscious of the fact that the existence of the back wound was a matter of which they did not have first-hand knowledge. It is of considerably greater interest, accordingly, to analyze the things they *did* see, rather than what they did not see. Both these doctors, unlike those who later contradicted them, had seen the throat wound of the President before the operation. That assumes immense importance from the fact that the incision for the operation to restore the patient's breathing was made in the very area that had already been laid open by the throat wound. The appearance of the wound was consequently altered, and the opening enlarged, before the body reached Bethesda— a fact which severely handicapped post mortem speculations. In an interview accorded to the St. Louis *Post Dispatch* reporter, Richard Dudman, Dr. McClelland "explained that he and his colleagues at Parkland saw bullet wounds every day, sometimes several a day, and recognized easily the characteristically tiny hole of an entering bullet, in contrast to the larger, tearing hole that an exiting bullet would have left." Both he and Dr. Perry said the wound in President Kennedy's throat conformed to the pattern of a bullet's entry. A dispatch from the New York *Herald Tribune* bureau to the Los Angeles *Times* November 24 described it this way: "The wound in the throat was small and neat."

The first-hand testimony of the Dallas doctors thus supports the view that the first shot was frontal, and one other element in the official evidence seems to indicate this. Motion picture film, confirming the eyewitness testimony, showed the President had grasped toward his throat, as though he felt that he was choking, after he was hit the first time. Yet the explanation that had been adopted when the President's Commission started its investigation—it will be recalled that this was, by this time, the *third* official version —held the throat wound to have been the last one. The first injury was said to have been in the shoulder.

This account of the location of the wounds and the shot sequence still prevailed officially when I discussed the case with the Deputy Attorney General of the United States in his office in the Department of Justice in March, 1964. I pointed out to Mr. Katzenbach that there appeared to be discrepancies in the account he gave me, but he said that it was based on an exhaustive study of the President's autopsy, and that there could be no doubt about it: That was how Bethesda doctors reconstructed the path of the bullets.

He felt certain any person who had studied this autopsy would have reached the same conclusions. I asked him if I could see a copy of it, but he said that he could not release it.

Six months later, when the President's Commission issued its report, the explanation of the wounds had changed completely, although it was still based on the same, unaltered medical report. The same authorities who were so certain of the previous interpretation now are equally sure of the new one.

The first shot, it is now said, hit the President in the back of the neck but did not remain, as the autopsy had first indicated, in the shoulder. It pursued a wholly altered course, emerging from the throat in a direct line. The next bullet entered Kennedy's skull at one point and is said to have emerged from the skull in another area, rather than through the throat, as first reported.

The pattern of the tissue damage does not, therefore, bear the least resemblance to the course of the two bullets that originally had been traced by the autopsy of the Bethesda doctors. If such diverse interpretations of a single document can be made, it must be so lacking in precision as to be completely worthless for the reconstruction of the crime.

Nothing that has subsequently been disclosed, in short, would furnish a convincing reason to discredit the conclusions of the chief neurosurgeon, Dr. Kemp Clark, who signed the official death certificate, or of his colleagues at Parkland Memorial Hospital. One may be permitted to express surprise at the suggestion that these men, whose whole careers have been devoted to reacting promptly and efficiently to an emergency, would have been so completely disconcerted by the fact the President was on the operating table that their judgment cannot be relied on. But if they were right in the beginning, then the whole official explanation of the crime collapses. For, in that case, the throat injury was, as they stated, caused by a shot fired from the front, and there are consequently two assassins.

*   *   *

THE OFFICIAL THESIS: That the marksman who fired all the shots was Oswald.

There are four compelling reasons to reject this theory. One of them—the great preponderance of evidence that shots were fired from opposite directions—would exclude the possibility that any single man fired all the bullets.

It must be excluded, likewise, by the fact that no one man can fire a 6.5 Carcano semi-automatic rifle with the speed required, since after each shot it not only must be manually loaded, but the moving target has to be again located in the telescopic sight and the exact lead to produce a hit recalculated. The greatest experts in the world, according to the President's Commission, would require a period of 2.3 seconds for each shot fired after the first one. And the President's Commission also states that the time interval between the two shots which produced the throat and skull wounds of the President was 4.8 to 5.6 seconds. It follows that if there was one shot in the period between them, it would have to have occurred precisely in the middle of this interval; if not, a second marksman fired it.

For the first six months of the investigation, after careful study of the motion picture of the series of events which had been filmed by a spectator, Abraham Zapruder, it was held to be established that the second shot had struck the Governor of Texas, and the Governor's own testimony had confirmed this. There was never any serious consideration to the possibility that both men had been wounded by a

93

single bullet, nor did Mr. Katzenbach suggest this when I interviewed him on the question.

What has caused the President's Commission to revise completely the official version of the wounds, deduced from the November 22nd autopsy, and the analysis of the trajectory of all the bullets, as provided in the F.B.I.'s original report of December, 1963?

It would appear that all these sweeping changes are impelled by the establishment as a conclusive fact that one or two shots fired November 22nd missed the target. There can be no further doubt on this point, which completely vindicates reporter Richard Dudman of the St. Louis *Post Dispatch*, whose stories that such evidence was found by the police had been described by the authorities as pure imagination. The Commission indicates in its report exactly where one bullet hit the street, and even names a witness who was injured by a ricocheting fragment. This shot went quite far from its intended target, hitting the south curb of Main Street, toward which the presidential car was heading. A spectator on the other side of Main Street, James T. Tague, felt something sting his cheek, which started bleeding. Deputy Sheriff Eddy R. Walthers and Dallas Patrolman L. L. Hill reported Tague was injured. Dallas Patrolman J. W. Foster asserted that there was a second bullet which had also missed its target, landing in the grass beside the underpass, but the Commission did not take this shot into consideration, since police said that the bullet had not been recovered.

That at least one bullet did not hit the President or the Governor, but missed completely, is therefore conceded by the President's Commission. The remaining bullets had produced two wounds in Kennedy and one in Connally. Thus, from the moment the Commission had conclusive evidence of the wild bullet, it was faced with a decision: Either there were four or five shots in too little time for one man to have fired them, or the three wounds were produced by two shots, and the rest went wild. The President's Commission chose the sole alternative that would not force it to admit that there were two assassins.

We are now asked to imagine that a bullet fired from the sixth floor hit Kennedy in the back, came out his throat in a new, flat trajectory, plunged into Connally's back and at once resumed its downward angle, shattering his fifth rib, then emerging from his chest with a velocity scarcely diminished, entering his wrist and passing through it, until finally it was embedded in his thigh. The car, at this time, was descending a grade of approximately 3 degrees, an insufficient angle to permit the relatively horizontal course from its first victim to its second unless it had been deflected by a bone as it passed through the body of the President. The President's Commission says, however, "No bone was struck by the bullet which passed through the President's body." The trajectory of the shot which hit Connally can be precisely measured from examination of his wounds. The President's Commission says its downward course was 25 degrees. A bullet falling at that angle could not possibly have struck the Governor's back only a few inches lower than the section of the President's back where it had previously entered. The trajectory is only plausible on the hypothesis of two deflections, one in each man's body, altering the bullet's course from vertical to nearly horizontal, then once more to vertical. Such changes in direction would imply the bullet twice struck something solid enough to deflect it. Contact with an obstacle of this type normally would slice a fragment from the bullet each time. Yet the bullet, after it had been recovered, was intact. It weighed 158.6 grains. The Commission says this type of ammunition weighs 160 to 161 grains, prior to firing.

This hypothesis—and the Commission has conceded that it is no more than that—can thus be shown to be exceedingly unlikely, even when it is presented as a "speculation." It must also be rejected on the basis of the testimony of the Governor of Texas and his wife, the most authoritative witnesses available. The Governor and Mrs. Connally agree that his wounds were not the result of any shot that hit the President. The Governor told the Commission that he heard the first shot, turned toward his right to see what happened, failed to find the source of the disturbance, heard the President cry out, and then turned in the opposite direction and saw the President's reaction to the throat wound when he was himself struck by a bullet that he did not hear. As he lay wounded, he heard at least one more shot and knew the President was hit again. He was, accordingly, quite certain that his own wound took place in the interval between the two that Kennedy had suffered, and the Governor denied that either of these bullets had hit him. The President's Commission, trying to avoid accepting the inevitable implication of this testimony that there were four shots, including one that missed, said in its report: "There was, conceivably, a delayed reaction between the time the bullet struck him and the time he realized that he was hit, despite the fact that the bullet struck a glancing blow to a rib and penetrated his wrist bone"—either of which clearly should have caused him instant pain, whereas mere flesh wounds may, in fact, remain unnoticed longer. No "delayed reaction" is attributable to his wife, who saw his body spun around against her by the bullet's impact. She confirmed his observation that this happened after she had turned and seen the President reach for his throat.

As has been stated by the President's Commission, no one in the world is capable of shooting three times with the murder weapon in a period of less than 4.6 seconds. Olympic rifle champion Hubert Hammerer has stated that he doubted whether any man alive could fire it accurately three times in 5 seconds. Yet the time between the President's two wounds has been established at from 4.8 to 5.6 seconds. It must be apparent that if the Governor of Texas and his wife are right, and there was one shot intervening, that shot would have to have been fired, as the report of the Commission pointed out, "almost exactly midway in this period." Does this, however, correspond with the Zapruder film, or with eyewitness testimony? It does not. For the report continued, "On the other hand, a substantial majority of the witnesses stated that the shots were not evenly spaced. Most witnesses recalled that the second and third shots were bunched together, although some believed that it was the first and second which were bunched."

The evidence is, therefore, overwhelming that two shots were fired at less than 2.3 seconds' interval from one another, which is the Commission's own criterion for the determination that the shots were fired by two men. When to this is added the fact that there was at least one more shot, in addition to the three already listed, it becomes apparent that the theory of a lone assassin is exploded, and no further proof is needed.

The shots came from two directions; their trajectory refutes the speculation that one shot hit both men; and no single marksman could have fired so quickly. These are three compelling reasons to reject the thesis that a lone assassin, posted on the sixth floor, killed the President unaided.

There is evidence, moreover, that Lee Oswald was not either of the two assassins. He did not possess the skill to fire the weapon with the accuracy that was demonstrated. Allowing for the vertical as well as lateral displacement of the target from the sixth-floor window, the first shot would have to have been fired from a range of more than 60 yards. This range would then have been increasing, for a marksman in the book depository, at a rate of about six yards per second, following the first shot. It is obvious, from the range alone, that the assassin's task was infinitely harder than that

97

of his predecessors who killed Lincoln, Garfield and Mc-Kinley, and yet Kennedy was wounded more severely than his predecessors. Lincoln lived nine hours after he was hit, McKinley eight days, Garfield 79 days; whereas Kennedy was dead in half an hour. Booth was only a few feet from Lincoln when he fired; Czolgosz was close enough to touch his victim; even Guiteau was no more than half the distance from which Kennedy's assassin fired.

Not only was the distance greater, but this was the first time that the victim had been moving while his murderer was firing, and *continued* moving after he was hit, but was then hit a second time. This means a lead was necessary, both in azimuth and elevation. Photographs have frequently been published, taken from the sixth-floor window, with the cross-hairs of a rifle sight superimposed upon a target on the street below. The caption of this picture often indicates that this would be an "easy target" to a marksman with a telescopic lens. It is worthwhile, in this connection, to remember that a shot aimed in that fashion would invariably miss the target, since the car was moving; the assassin had to aim above his target and to his right. No matter how precise the weapon he was using, firing of this type requires the judgment of an expert, in order to anticipate precisely where the target will be when the bullet gets there.

The murder weapon was a rifle with a telescopic sight and a bolt action which must be pulled back by hand after each shot, in order to reload it. Such a weapon is designed for snipers, and is meant for single shots, and not for rapid firing. Fully automatic rifles can be held against a moving object and the marksman, though compelled by each shot's recoil to adjust his aim, remains close to his target. With a telescopic sight, the problem is more complicated, since the lens limits the marksman's field of vision and it takes longer for him to locate his target, especially if it is moving. But when the bolt must be pulled back by hand each time a shot is fired, the time lost in recovering the target is considerably greater. It may thus be stated that if four shots were fired, no single marksman in the world was capable of this achievement; that if any two of the shots came within 2.3 seconds of each other, this would also be conclusive proof that there were two marksmen; and that even if there were three shots, evenly spaced, not more than one skilled marksman in a thousand could have fired them accurately in the time required.

Was the official suspect, Lee H. Oswald, capable of this performance? Here, we have a solid basis for evaluating Oswald's capability; we have his service record. This completely contradicts the references which have frequently been made to Oswald's reputation as a "crack shot." Not all veterans of the Marines are expert riflemen. *The New York Times* observed November 23rd, "Lee Harvey Oswald was not highly regarded as a rifleman." That was an understatement. According to the President's Commission, Oswald's service record indicates the last time that he took a qualifying test in marksmanship, he scored 191 points of a possible 250. This took place in 1959, after three years of military service—that is to say, when Oswald had presumably learned all that the Marines could teach him. Such a score is based on 50 shots, with 5 points for a bull's-eye, 4 for the nearest of a series of concentric circles, 3 for the next, and so forth. Only a small number of these shots are fired, as the assassin had to, in the comparatively difficult kneeling rapid-fire position. Many shots are made with no time limit, and some from the relatively easy prone position. I have been through basic military training of this type three times myself—once as a soldier in the Army Air Corps, once as an officer candidate, and for three years with men whom I commanded in an automatic weapons unit. Of those men whom I have witnessed or have personally trained, 95 percent scored better, in the first few months of service, than Oswald did when he was fully trained and so, presumably, as good as he would ever be. Most men do as' well as 191 the first time that they ever fire a rifle. *All* men are required to make a certain minimum score—which, in this case, was 190—no matter how many attempts it takes them. If a man does not achieve this level on his first try, he is given special coaching and his officer is forced to march him out each day and stay there with him at the rifle range until one time, by luck or cheating, the unhappy wretch succeeds in meeting the requirement. The Baltimore *Sun* of November 24th noted, "A marine officer at the Pentagon suggested today that the low score indicated he might have failed the first qualifying test and had to make a second try." Lest it be thought that Oswald simply had bad luck that day, it may be added that the best score that he ever made, in three years of Marine-trained target practice, was 212—which is still lower than the average for men in his branch of the service. He was given a "sharpshooter" rating for that mediocre effort. Persons unfamiliar with American medals may be impressed by this; the fact is, though, that "sharpshooter" is the intermediate class between "expert" and "marksman"—a "marksman" designation being the lowest acceptable category, in which Oswald habitually fell. It will be seen, therefore, that in Oswald's best effort, he was barely able to attain the level of the lowest portion of the middle group.

Nelson Delgado, specialist fourth class in the Army, who had served in the Marines with Oswald, testified April 16th before staff counsel Wesley J. Liebeler of the President's Commission in regard to Oswald's marksmanship. Dom Bonafede of the New York *Herald Tribune* read a transcript of this testimony, which he summarized June 14th in these terms: "The accused slayer of President Kennedy was such a poor shot while in the Marines that it became 'a pretty big joke.' " Delgado stated further that he had related to the F.B.I. that even when a group of Marines set up an informal contest, with five prizes for the highest scorers in a group of 40, Oswald's marksmanship did not improve, and he remembered noticing how many times Oswald's shots kicked up the dust and did not even hit the target's outer ring, so that Oswald was frequently the victim of the serviceman's worst ignominy—waving of the flag called "Maggie's drawers," which indicates the shot has missed completely. The ex-corporal in the Marines said that the F.B.I. men "badgered" him in "what he believed was an attempt to distort the nature of his testimony," and he got the clear impression they were discontented to find out that Oswald was a poor shot. They interrogated him on four separate occasions, he asserted. F.B.I. officials, told of Delgado's allegations, refused to comment.

It is therefore evident that Oswald was, throughout the period in which he may be reasonably thought to have been at the peak of his ability to fire a rifle, one of the worst shots in the Marines—or, for that matter, any other military service. To suppose that he shot better after four years of civilian life is perfectly fantastic; shooting, more than any other sport, takes practice. Weeks after the President was murdered, vague reports were published that Oswald had been seen repeatedly, driving a car into a rifle range for target practice. The Commission denies that such reports are valid. One compelling reason for this disavowal is that Oswald could not drive a car; he had just started taking lessons. Even if he had been trained in secret by an expert far superior to his Marine instructors—and this supposition, in itself, implies complicity in the assassination by the man who trained him—I have never seen a man improve that much, once he has been subjected to his basic training, and I doubt if anybody else has. When a certain level of ability in such a skill has been established, further practice yields diminishing returns.

The problem Kennedy's assassin faced was far more complicated than mere target practice. Kennedy was riding in a car which, the report says, had been moving at 11.2 miles an hour, the equivalent of 6 yards in a second, only slightly less than the top speed at which a man is capable of running. By the time the last shot had been fired, this speed had certainly increased. It would thus correspond with the most difficult of targets that a soldier would encounter under battlefield conditions. Target practice of the type shown on the Oswald service record is fired at a stationary target, and does not require the calculation of a lead. Oswald, of course, had no experience in combat. Nor is there much likelihood that Oswald, during his Marine days, fired a foreign weapon of the same type he is charged with shooting, and one wonders why he would have chosen such an unfamiliar type of rifle for his own use. He, no doubt, was given training with a U. S. Springfield rifle which, like the Italian carbine—a 6.5 mm. Carcano—has a bolt which must be pulled back after each shot. But it is not likely that, in ordinary training, Oswald (who was not primarily a rifleman but a communications clerk) received instruction on a weapon with a telescopic sight. For a man who had not ever fired one, it would require considerable adaptation.

It is doubtful if a single man exists who could have fired this weapon with the skill required. But if the feat is possible it is, in the opinion of the experts, a superlative performance which requires one of the world's best marksmen.

*　　　*　　　*

THE OFFICIAL THESIS: The police have proved by scientific evidence that Oswald fired the murder weapon.

It was said, at first, that the police had found the fingerprints of Oswald on the rifle. In the second version, Oswald's "fingerprints" were changed to "palmprints" by District Attorney Henry Wade. In April, Allen Dulles, former C.I.A. chief and a member of the President's Commission, reinstated the original assertion that Lee Oswald's fingerprints were on the rifle—but he added, almost casually, the most damaging avowal that has yet been made upon this question. He announced, without elaboration, that "the murder weapon bore, *among others,* fingerprints of Oswald."

The report of the Commission merely states that "Oswald's palmprint on the underside of the barrel demonstrates that he handled the rifle when it was disassembled. A palmprint could not be placed on this portion of the rifle, when assembled, because the wooden foregrip covers the barrel at this point. The print is additional proof that the rifle was in Oswald's possession." No prints were, however, found that would show Oswald had been holding the Carcano when it was last used. That the man who owned the rifle should have left his fingerprints upon it while he disassembled it and cleaned it is not too surprising—and, in fact, the absence of such prints would have been more incriminating than their presence; it would indicate that after he had cleaned his rifle, he removed them. But the question that cries out for answer is: Who else had left his fingerprints upon it? The report submitted by the President's Commission does not give the answer. It says merely that the testimony of F.B.I. expert Sebastian F. Latona was "that the latent prints which were there were of no value."

Oswald's prints were also found on cardboard cartons in the stockroom where the murderer is said to have been standing. This could scarcely be regarded as conclusive, since he had free access to the room and moving boxes there was part of his legitimate and normal function. Evidence of this sort would, in any case, convict him of complicity in preparation of the crime, but it would tend to prove he did not actually fire the rifle. For if he left prints upon the cartons just before the crime, it means he had no gloves on. And if Oswald was not wearing gloves at that time, and he was the last to touch the rifle, then he would have left a number of clear fingerprints upon it—for, as will be shown, he could not possibly have had the time to wipe prints off the rifle after he had fired it.

The Police Department's second scientific test tends, likewise, to disprove their thesis rather than confirm it. They subjected Oswald to a paraffin test after his arrest to find out if he had just fired a weapon. The result was positive—it showed gunpowder on his hands, but none on his cheeks. District Attorney Wade himself conceded this point, though he did so indirectly. He told news reporters, "I've got tests that showed he had recently fired a gun—it was on both hands." The word "gun," to men familiar with the use of weapons, cannot be applied to rifles, but to *pistols*. Oswald had, indeed, possessed a pistol when police arrested him; it is the weapon said to have been used in the subsequent murder of a Dallas policeman; it is not the weapon used to kill the President. If Oswald fired at the policeman with his pistol, that, of course, explains the powder on his hands; but why was powder absent from his cheek, if he had also fired a rifle with a telescopic sight? A reporter, anxious to make certain he had not misquoted Wade, asked him again if he had not intended to say that the paraffin test proved Oswald had just fired a *rifle*. Wade repeated the same word, without explaining its significance—"a gun," he stated.

I have subsequently seen, and am now looking at, a copy of the report sent to the District Attorney's office by the

Dallas City-County Criminal Investigation Laboratory. The analyst, Louis L. Anderson, states that he received the following "specimen" from the Dallas police: Exhibit 1, "One manila envelope containing a paraffin cast of the right side of the face of Lee Oswald"; Exhibit 2, "One manila envelope containing a paraffin cast of the left hand of Lee Oswald"; and Exhibit 3, "One manila envelope containing a paraffin cast of the right hand of Lee Oswald." The "result of examination" is given in these words, which I have reproduced in their entirety: "No nitrates were found on Exhibit 1. Nitrate patterns consistent with the subject having discharged a firearm were present on Exhibits 2 and 3. The pattern on Exhibit 3 is typical of the patterns produced in firing a revolver."

When I was in Washington in March, I raised this question with the Deputy Attorney General. Mr. Nicholas De B. Katzenbach admitted to me that it was a gap in the case against Oswald which he could not explain.

That efforts have been made to fill this gap by casting doubts on the validity of the Dallas laboratory report (as on the report of the Dallas surgeons) is now apparent. The report of the President's Commission says the paraffin test was considered to be "inconclusive," and a second test was subsequently made, subjecting the same paraffin to a new, allegedly more sensitive technique called "activation analysis" which a California company has been trying to sell to criminal laboratories. It led to no definite incrimination, either. How much time elapsed between the two tests has not been announced, but it is hard to see how the same paraffin casts could have been reused. In the report of the Dallas Criminal Investigation Laboratory, which I have before me, there is a form to be filled out which states what the laboratory has done with the specimen after the test was finished. It was not returned to the police, according to the laboratory's signed report; it was "discarded."

The third test, relating to the clothing fragments said to have been found upon the rifle, tends to show that Oswald brought it to the building. It casts no light on the fundamental question: Did he fire it?

No gunpowder traces were embedded in the suspect's cheek. His fingerprints were found only upon a portion of the weapon that he could not have touched while firing. Apart from the proofs already given, indicating the improbability that Oswald had the skill to fire the murder weapon, it must be considered that a suspect who has neither held a rifle in his hand nor pressed it up against his cheek is quite unlikely to have fired the rifle.

*   *   *

THE OFFICIAL THESIS: Oswald, who did not work normally upon the sixth floor though he often used the stockroom, waited for his fellow workers to leave on their noon-hour lunch break, then went up to the sixth floor and remained alone there in the stockroom until the motorcade turned into Elm Street.

In the first official version, he was said to have spent part of his time eating. *Four Days,* the widely sold book rushed out after the assassination, says, "The sniper had dined on fried chicken and pop while waiting patiently to shoot the President." This was, in fact, what Captain Will Fritz, chief of homicide in the Dallas police force, had advised the nation, in a television interview. But Roy S. Truly later told authorities the chicken bones and carbonated beverage had been consumed by Bonnie Ray Williams, one of five employees of the book depository who had been assigned to work all morning in the very room from which the shots are said to have been fired, laying plywood upon the floor. According to the report which it has published, the President's Commission has accepted this explanation and does not believe that Oswald ate the chicken.

Also found, near the bag that contained the chicken, was an empty cigarette pack. It would not be easy to attribute this to Oswald's presence. I quote now from *Time* magazine, December 6th: "Oswald was driven by a storm of black compulsions. . . . A non-smoker and teetotaler, he flew into rages when his wife lit a cigarette."

No eyewitness has, in fact, placed Oswald definitely in the stockroom just before the murder. Yet there has been testimony that a figure was observed there just before the motorcade went past. According to a twenty-year-old part-time college student who appeared in March before the President's Commission, he saw someone with a rifle on the sixth floor of the book depository, while he waited for the President to come past, but did not give the alarm, assuming it was just a Secret Service agent. He said he could not identify the man, but he was sure of one thing— that the man he saw was not where Oswald is reported to have waited, by the southeast corner window. The man with the rifle was in the same room, but at the southwest corner.

*   *   *

THE OFFICIAL THESIS: Oswald's actions in the first few moments after the assassination are described as follows: He first hid the rifle, then rushed down the hallway to the other end of the building where the stairway was located, hurried down four flights of stairs, went into the canteen, and he was found there, on the second floor, by his boss, Roy S. Truly, who had run upstairs with a policeman.

Time describes it this way, in its issue of December 6th:

> After he fired, Oswald ran toward the center of the building and down an aisle to a stairwell door. There, behind a few boxes of books, he thrust his carbine. He then hurried down the steps—and perhaps because he heard the oncoming footsteps of the motorcycle cop and Superintendent Truly—he ducked quickly into the lunchroom.

Meanwhile, *Time* says:

> Just after the presidential car sped off, Warehouse Superintendent Roy S. Truly, who had just stepped outside his building into the sideline crush of well wishers on Elm Street, saw a motorcycle cop running through the crowd, knocking people out of the way as he made for the door of the warehouse. Truly joined him, led him to the elevator. An upstairs elevator gate was open, immobilizing the whole system. Truly bounded up a staircase with the cop behind him, his revolver drawn. Off the second-floor landing the cop saw a lunchroom. He ran inside, saw a man standing next to a Coke machine. It was Lee Harvey Oswald. The cop asked Truly: "This boy work here?" Truly said yes. At that the officer wheeled and ran up the steps, somehow convinced that any sniper in the building must be a stranger and not an employee.

Since the time element is a decisive factor, it is most important to hear Truly's own description of the time it took before he first saw Oswald, after the assassination. He told Leo Sauvage, the distinguished correspondent of the right-wing Paris paper *Le Figaro:* "It was as soon as the last shot was fired when I saw the officer come running. As a matter of fact, it was so soon afterward that I don't believe he was riding in the motorcade. He must have been off his motorcycle, standing nearby. Anyway, it was right away after the shots. I knew they were shots, but had no idea they were fired from the building. I thought the officer wanted to get to the roof for a better look and I immediately offered to show him how. We ran to the freight elevators in the back of the building because the front elevators do not go beyond the fourth floor, but the two freight cars had both been left somewhere on the top floors and we took the stairs, the officer ahead of me. When I reached the second-floor landing, the officer was already at the door of the lunchroom, some twenty or twenty-five feet away. . . . I couldn't tell you exactly how much time it took, all this, but it wasn't long."

The first place within the building that was searched was, consequently, the canteen, and we have what, according to official sources, was a footrace—neither having used the elevator—between Oswald, who descended from the sixth floor, and the first policeman who rushed in the building, who ran up one flight of stairs to reach the second floor. Each man made one detour. Oswald took time to get rid of his rifle, and the other lost a few seconds waiting for the elevator. They began their race almost at the same moment—"just after the presidential car sped off"— yet by the time the officer had climbed one floor, the murderer is said to have descended four flights—and he was not even breathing deeply! Nor did Oswald seem excited, after his alleged mad dash to the canteen, and Roy S. Truly, who knew Oswald well, is quoted in the New York *Herald Tribune* of November 25th:

> The policeman threw a gun into Oswald's stomach and asked me if Oswald belonged there. I told him "yes" and we both went on up the stairs for a check of other floors. Oswald looked a bit startled—just as you or I would if someone suddenly threw a gun on you—but he didn't appear too nervous nor panicky.

Oswald must, according to this thesis, be not only a more accurate and rapid shot than the Olympic rifle champion, but the fastest runner since the great Olympic title holder, Jesse Owens.

THE official thesis that the murderer was Oswald, and that Oswald managed to perform the crime unaided, thus depends upon a chain of circumstances which are independent of each other, to which we may now assign the degree of credibility we think they warrant. Each of these assumptions is essential to the thesis that Lee Oswald was the lone assassin and, if any link is broken, the official explanation will collapse completely.

At this point, if I conceived my function to be that of a defense attorney for Lee Harvey Oswald, I should rest my case and leave it to the reader to decide if there is reasonable doubt that Oswald killed the President of the United States. Each of us has a rendezvous with his own conscience on this matter. For my own part, I am not in doubt and, if I were a member of the jury, I should vote: Not Guilty.

This, however, is a book and not a courtroom argument. A lawyer who defends his client is not obligated to explain what happened; he is satisfied to show the crime was not committed in the way the state's attorney had described it. I conceive an author's task to go beyond this. I believe that in a book based on a crime which changed the course of history a writer is a special kind of witness, and that where his path is blocked by shadows he must try to grope beyond them. He must do what any courtroom judge would find abhorrent; he must speculate on matters that are not part of his firsthand knowledge.

It would be astonishing, indeed, if the hypothesis that follows were correct, in its minutest detail. I regard it as no more than the most logical deduction from the facts which the investigating agencies have, thus far, made known to the public. It was their responsibility to make sure of these facts in the beginning, or preserve their silence. Each time that new data have been introduced, or the description of the data previously known was altered, the revision has been given due consideration. If there are some changes in my own views, which had been originally published in most European countries and Japan in February, March and April, 1964, it is because an analyst of this crime is compelled, like the assassins, to fire on a moving target. Nor is there assurance that all the known facts have been revealed yet, or will be disclosed "within our lifetime." The remark of Murray Kempton in the *New Republic* June 13th is pertinent to this point: "There is something uncomfortably petty about a man who locks up a document and then complains about the ignorance of another man because he hasn't read it."

The foregoing portion of the book, as has been stated, was based on analysis of the official version of the crime, on its inherent logic or illogic. The remaining section will make use not only of the facts announced by the police, but equally of the research of hundreds of reporters, both in the United States and Europe, and of interviews in Dallas by private correspondents who have sent me the results of their own personal investigation.

The hypothesis that follows is, accordingly, a synthesis of many people's contributions. Let it not be thought of as a final formulation of the author's outlook. It is certainly not that. Let it be thought of as a mere beginning. For this is the kind of issue which cannot be carried to its resolution by the work of any one man or small group of individuals. The responsibility is shared by all the citizens of the United States to learn the truth about the murder of the man who led them. In the measure that this formidable labor comes to be collective, there is hope that it may, in the end, be fruitful.

*　　　　*　　　　*

Until now, we have been dealing with the possibility of one or more accomplices, and Oswald's total innocence is not, as yet, excluded. Two men, we have reason to assume, came into the sixth-floor stockroom of the book depository some time between noon, when the work detail left, and the assassination, half an hour later. Their admission, separately or together, was not ever challenged, for two reasons: First, employees of the book depository had their luncheon break from noon until 12:45, and most of them had gone out on the street to watch the President go by; and second, there was no police control of the school book depository building. It was not searched, and accordingly it is quite possible that one or more men came into the stockroom from outside the building. There is no proof that Lee Oswald was there, although I am very much inclined to think he was. Of the various eyewitnesses who said they saw a figure on the sixth floor either during or before the crime, there is not one who was positively able to identify Lee Oswald. But if facts not heretofore disclosed confirm his presence, it is clear from all the reasons previously cited that his role was that of an accomplice. Who was the assassin? We know only that this man was probably in a profession where he was accustomed to the use of foreign weapons, and engaged in frequent target practice. We may also say that the profession giving him free access to the building at this time, even if he were noticed by a company official, would be that of a policeman. We may now identify him as Assassin Two, since he is not the one who fired the first shot.

Meanwhile, the man destined to become Assassin One was walking down the railroad tracks that start at Union Station, opposite the Dallas *Morning News* building, and cross the triple underpass, then wind behind the book depository. After walking a few hundred yards beside the tracks, Assassin One now crossed the bridge and stood there, just like any other citizen who climbs a tree or crawls out on a roof to get an unobstructed view of the parade. If he encountered a policeman on the way, then it must be assumed that this assassin was a man on good terms with the whole police force, someone who would never be suspected of a plan to kill the President of the United States, a man whose petty violations of the law had never gotten him into much trouble and who, if the need arose, could certainly have talked his way past a NO TRESPASSING sign on the day the President was driving by.

So Assassins One and Two were waiting. . . . And, at last, the presidential car came into view, turned right from Main Street into Houston and was coming straight toward the sixth-floor window of the Texas School Book Depository. If Assassin Two, the man who had been hiding in the stockroom, had been all alone, now was the moment that he would have chosen for his first shot—now, before the car had turned the corner and begun receding. But the moment passed, and Kennedy drove on toward the ambush that was waiting. As the car descended Elm Street, headed for the railway overpass, Assassin Two's view temporarily was hampered by a tree between him and his target, but it did not matter. For Assassin One, by this time, had unwrapped his rifle. Crouching by the concrete wall, he pointed its black muzzle through one of the deep slits spaced throughout its length. His body would have shielded it from anybody who was not beside him, and his neighbors would have rushed for vantage points along the wall, as the parade drew near. It is a long wall, spanning three streets and continuing beyond them, chest high but with solid portions rising to a height of eight feet at repeated intervals, dividing the wall into sections. People leaning over this wall could not possibly have seen a man crouched down in an adjoining section, nor was the policeman there in a position to survey their movements. To do that, he would have had to have been standing on the far side of the bridge, behind them. But as the parade drew near, the officer apparently moved forward, and a Secret Service agent, Winston G. Lawson, testified that the policeman was so close to the wall that he saw him from the street below and tried in vain to get him to prevent spectators from assembling just above where Kennedy's car would be passing. A policeman who had stood behind these people would not have been visible from a car in the street below.

As the President's car drew near, Assassin One saw the chauffeur in the front seat, then the Governor of Texas and his wife, who occupied the middle seat, and in the third and rear seat, on the left, he saw his target. And he squeezed the trigger.

In the car, still coming down the hill toward the murderer, John Fitzgerald Kennedy now grasped his throat, where the first bullet entered, and his wife moaned, "Oh, my God, they have shot my husband! I love you, Jack...." The President of the United States was dying.

On the bridge, Assassin One now flung the weapon from him. On the street below him, near the spot where Kennedy was shot, a number of eyewitnesses had turned toward the bridge from which the bullet seemed to have been fired. An instant later, though, a second shot rang out—and from the opposite direction. It was fired by the assassin in the book depository, and it missed its target, but it served the purpose for which it had been intended: to create the indispensable diversion while Assassin One was fleeing. The spectators on the bridge stood by the wall, their eyes upon the scene before them. They would not have noticed anyone who ran along the tracks behind them. The policeman who was meant to guard the east end of the bridge, J. W. Foster, was not in a position where he could have noticed, either. As soon as he heard the first shot, he told the President's Commission, he "rushed to the wall of the railroad bridge over the Triple Underpass and looked toward the street." And the report continued, "After the third shot, Foster ran toward the Depository"—that is to say, toward the west end of the bridge, leaving the east end unguarded. There was, accordingly, no officer of the police to stop a person running east toward the railroad station. Were there such people? That is the opinion of reliable reporters in the motorcade, who saw a man and woman fleeing from the bridge in that direction. This report was broadcast to the nation, in the first few minutes after the assassination. It is not invalidated by the fact that no such persons volunteered to testify before the President's Commission. A policeman, Clyde A. Haygood, did, in fact, run up the grassy slope toward the railway tracks at the Book Depository end of the bridge, but by the time he reached the top he says that he saw no one running down the tracks. The pursuit was therefore thwarted, and since shots continued from the book depository, it was totally abandoned.

One may speculate now as to the direction in which the assassin on the bridge was running. It would seem unlikely that he would have run away from Union Station, since the tracks in that direction bend toward the book depository where policemen were converging. Thus he was compelled to run toward the station. He could not have scrambled down the embankment on the far side of the bridge, for he would thereby have exposed himself to the immediate view of cars preceding Kennedy's in the parade.

He could not very well have run directly in the station, where he would have certainly been seen. But there is one place where, within a minute, he could have contrived to disappear completely: the long warehouse between the post office and the Union Station passenger terminal. Entering the open side, next to the railroad tracks, he could have run through the building and emerged on Houston Street. The elapsed time would now be two minutes. He would find himself beside the waiting rooms of Union Station—but since he would now be panting and conspicuous, he certainly would not have gone in there where someone would be sure to see him. Nor could he have turned left on Houston and gone back to Main Street, where police were gathered. He could have crossed Houston Street and fled across the park, but since the trees there offer no concealment that would seem a dangerous procedure. He could not have turned right and traversed the viaduct, for since no pedestrians are allowed there any person walking or running beside the cars would have been most conspicuous. A high official of the Justice Department has suggested to me that a fleeing murderer from the bridge—an hypothesis he does not officially admit—might have had a car parked beside the railway terminal, and fled by motor. But if he did not, then there is only one remaining alternative: to run diagonally across Houston Street into one of the side entrances of the Dallas *Morning News,* a building almost totally deserted, since its employees had gone down Houston Street to Main Street to see Kennedy go by. Assassin One could then remain there until he had caught his breath and had regained composure, and find some legitimate excuse for being there. The whole trip would have taken him three minutes at a brisk trot or, at normal walking pace, not more than five or six. I timed it, while I was in Dallas during the Jack Ruby trial. I might add that the warehouse, during the lunch hour when I made the test, was empty. All its doors were open.

Testimony at the Ruby trial confirmed what journalists already had reported—that Jack Ruby had been at the Dallas *Morning News* before and after the assassination. He had been preparing advertising copy for his strip-tease club. Considering that he has been described as having had an adoration for the man he now calls "our beloved President" that bordered on insanity—indeed, which passed that border—one regrets the press of business affairs which prevented him that day from taking a few minutes to go down and watch his hero pass, just a few hundred yards away. Ruby explained it this way to Chief Justice Warren, in the jail interview of which Dorothy Kilgallen published the transcript: "I will state why I didn't go to the parade. In the first place, I don't want to go where there is big crowds. I can't explain it to you. If I was interested, I would have seen it on television."

The last man who saw Jack Ruby at the *Morning News* before the President's assassination is reported to have been Donald Campbell, who left him there about 12:20. This would be ten minutes prior to the crime. Jack Ruby now remained alone, with only a few sentences to write for the small ad that he intended placing, and no one to disturb him or to talk to. He was still there when John Newman entered at about 12:45, a quarter of an hour after the assassination. Although all police cars in a radius of many miles had been converging, with their sirens wailing, on the book depository—which Jack Ruby could have seen, down Houston Street, by looking out the window— Ruby did not ask John Newman what had happened. It appears to have been someone else who told him. The French paper *Libération*, in its issue of November 27th, quoted Newman as having told reporters: "I heard someone shout, 'The President has been shot!' They think the

117

man who fired at him is hiding in this building!" At this news, said Newman, Ruby seemed "extremely upset."

*   *   *

Although it was manifestly possible for an assassin on the bridge to reach a place of safety, it is not conceivable that he would have run, carrying his weapon with him. He must, therefore, have discarded it upon the bridge, or near it. The police would then inevitably have retrieved it. Is there any indication that a second rifle was in fact discovered? Evidence to this effect is overwhelming. It would be sufficient in itself to refute the official theory of a lone assassin.

I am looking at a photostatic copy of the most authoritative statement on this matter that can be produced—the signed report, dated November 23, 1963, of Seymour Weitzman, the Dallas policeman who was credited with having found the rifle in the book depository. He declared, "This rifle was a 7.65 Mauser bolt action equipped with a 4/18 * scope, a thick leather brownish-black sling on it. The rifle was between some boxes near the stairway. The time the rifle was found was 1:22 P.M. Captain Fritz took charge of the rifle and ejected one live round from the chamber."

The description of the weapon by Policeman Weitzman is, as would have been expected in a case of this importance, a detailed, precise one. It precludes the possibility that his examination was so superficial that he made the error of confusing an Italian Carcano with a German

* The scope size is almost illegible upon this photostat, and I cannot be certain that the figure is correctly cited.

Mauser, or mistook a weapon of 6.5 caliber for the much larger 7.65.

Weitzman's statement is supported by the judgment of the motorcycle officer who had been riding near the President, B. W. Hargis. He told the Dallas *Times Herald* November 22nd, "They found the rifle and took it to have it fingerprinted. An immediate investigation was begun on the gun's origin. It looked to me like a Mauser."

Finally, the weapon found in the school book depository was sent to District Attorney Henry Wade. He told news reporters without any qualifying statement that it was a German Mauser. An assertion of this sort is not based on opinion, nor does it require a laboratory test of any sort in order to confirm it. Henry Wade, as those reporters who attended the Jack Ruby trial will testify, sometimes takes pleasure posing as a bumbling and confused provincial, but he is in fact a very shrewd man who for fourteen years has been District Attorney, and served as an agent for the F.B.I. for four years. His experience should, therefore, have prepared him to distinguish a Carcano from a Mauser.

It has been contended that, "in the confusion," Henry Wade and Weitzman made an error in identifying a Carcano as a Mauser, though the two, it is conceded, do not much resemble one another. It must be assumed, however, that both men can read. Upon the weapon now in the possession of the President's Commission, written in large letters which had been engraved upon the rifle by the firm that made it, and which would have been one of the first things any person glancing at it would observe, are the words MADE ITALY and the additional marking, CAL 6.5.

This fact can be verified by reference to page 83 of the report of the President's Commission, in the picture of Exhibit 541(3). It shows beyond all reasonable contradiction that the weapon found by Weitzman could not have

119

been the Carcano. Weitzman, like the Dallas surgeons, was correct from the beginning.

The authorities in Dallas have informed us solemnly that Kennedy was murdered by a Mauser. The men who made this first statement were all competent to practice their profession. I believe them. They informed us later that the President was killed by a Carcano. I believe that, also. I am forced to the conclusion that there were two weapons. I deduce that there were two assassins.

*   *   *

If, as now seems likely, the assassin in the book depository used the Mauser that Policeman Weitzman found there, where did the Carcano come from? That appears to have been Oswald's function. Oswald's neighbor and co-worker, Wesley Frazier, told investigators that he drove Oswald to work the morning of November 22nd. He said Oswald had a package. Oswald told him there were curtain rods inside it. There has been no evidence which would disprove this, and it is a fact that the small rented room Oswald had taken did need curtains. On the other hand, Marina Oswald has confirmed the allegation that her husband did possess a rifle similar to that one which the President's Commission has been given as "the" murder weapon, and it disappeared that morning from the place where it was hidden—the garage of Ruth Paine, with whom Oswald's family was living.

Frazier is, to date, the only person at the book depository who has said that he saw Oswald with this package. If, indeed, it was a rifle, Oswald does not seem to have incurred the risk of carrying it upstairs with him as he checked in to his job that morning. There is no proof that Oswald delivered it, in person, or that this is what had been intended. He could much more safely have left it at a designated spot where someone else would come by later for it. Several intruders, not employed at the depository, were in fact observed inside the private parking lot a short time prior to the President's assassination, I have learned from private sources. Some of them drove off in a car bearing stickers of a politician hostile to the President. The book depository parking lot, it should be noted, is set back from Elm Street, out of sight of passing traffic. One side of it runs along the railroad track next to the bridge across the overpass, from where witnesses say they heard the first shot.

This would seem, then, to provide a likely answer to the question: Where did the assassin on the bridge obtain his weapon, and in what way did he manage to conceal it?

A reporter for a Dallas paper, usually well informed, denied that Weitzman is the man who first saw the Carcano rifle. In a conversation with a private source, he stated that Captain Fritz, mentioned in the Weitzman report as having taken charge of the reputed murder weapon, was not present either. He asserted that two other men found the Carcano, one of them a sheriff's deputy whom he identified, and he said this man took the rifle to the sheriff's office.

This reporter, following official explanations, naturally took for granted that the weapon had been found in the school book depository, but when he asked his informant to tell him exactly where he found it, "his first reports were sort of confused." It has frequently been noted that the location where the rifle was discovered has been subject to considerable contradiction, which continued long after the "confusion" of the first few days. The possibility can certainly not be excluded that if the Carcano had been found outside the building, it could have been brought in later—from the railroad yards, for instance. "Minutes after the assassination," the Dallas *Times Herald* reported December 8th, "officers swarmed railroad yards near the assassination scene. A man was reported seen in that area carrying a rifle."

Similar confusion must have reigned if two policemen did, in fact, rush breathlessly back to headquarters, each one brandishing what he proclaimed to be the "murder weapon." The first choice seems to have been the Mauser. But on soberer consideration, after it was learned from F.B.I. files that Lee Oswald owned a 6.5 Carcano, the decision was awarded to the latter, and the German weapon vanished from consideration.

If, in fact, there had been no more than one murder weapon, and the error in identifying it was the result of one man's hasty glance, it is apparent that this error would have been corrected by the first policeman who gave it a thorough check—by Captain Fritz, for instance, or by any other officer at the Police Headquarters. Such an error could not possibly have lasted more than a few minutes. It could not have been repeated all day long by the District Attorney, Henry Wade. Nor is there any hint of doubt in the report signed by Policeman Weitzman, whose reaffirmation that the weapon was a Mauser was made November 23rd, a whole day later. This can no longer be attributed to the confusion of the moment. It is evident the explanation must go deeper.

*　　　*　　　*

It has been suggested that the first assassin managed to escape when his accomplice started firing from the book depository. How, then, did Assassin Two contrive to get down from the sixth floor and to leave the building?

That police were able to have blocked all exits by the

time he reached them may be proved beyond all doubt. Even the official version concedes Oswald could get no farther than the second floor. Police Chief Curry, as was previously noted, was himself outside the building when the shots were fired, since he had led the motorcade. Thus no excuse of panic or the absence of responsible officials at the scene can be advanced as explanation for the manner in which that search was conducted. It was under the direct command of the police chief from the very outset. Nor was there the slightest hesitation in identifying the precise location of the building on which the police were to converge. Police Chief Curry, whose own vehicle was not far from the railway overpass when the first shot was fired, said he could tell at once that all the shots came from the book depository. Moments after the assassination, therefore, he had radioed instructions to police upon the scene and all those in the neighborhood—he says 500 men responded—to surround and search that building. Any officers who had been heading for the railroad tracks were, like the officer already quoted, halted by the sound of "someone" shouting to them to go back toward the book depository. To suppose that the assassin came down from the sixth floor of that building and got out of the door before police controlled the exits is beyond all credibility. The building stood alone, and could at once have been surrounded. Any man who left it must have done what Oswald did—walked out of the door past uniformed policemen. I suggest the man who had the best chance of accomplishing this feat would have been someone who was wearing that same uniform himself. But there was no necessity for him to leave the building, for if he was in the uniform of a policeman he could easily have stayed within the book depository, blending inconspicuously with his fellow officers in the pursuit of the assassin. Such a man could have escaped unnoticed.

Meanwhile, upstairs on the second floor stood Oswald.

If he was, indeed, involved in the conspiracy, his fellow plotters may have told him that the rifle he delivered was to be used by somebody on the bridge. He may not have suspected shots were fired from his own building; that would certainly have been more risky for him. He appears to have been confident that he was too far from the crime to be suspected, and that by the time suspicion was directed at him, he would have escaped from danger.

He passed his first test with complete success when Roy S. Truly and the motorcycle officer rushed up to him in the canteen, although if he had not had reason to suppose that he was safe it would have seemed to him at that time that the game was up and he had been arrested. (His behavior later in the movie theatre in which he was captured was in total contrast; there, knowing he was all alone now, Oswald seemed to panic.) After this escape, one might have thought that Oswald would not hesitate, but hurry from the building, on the chance that it had not yet been surrounded. On the contrary, he bought a carbonated drink before departing. *Time* reported it this way:

> Carrying his Coke, Oswald ambled into a nearby office. A switchboard operator * said, "Wasn't that terrible—the President being shot?" Oswald mumbled something unintelligible, went out of the office, walked down the steps and slipped through the crowd outside.

Does it seem plausible to any reader that police let people leave a building when a search is going on inside it for the man who killed the President of the United States? It did not to U. E. Baughman, who for thirteen years had the responsibility, as chief of the Secret Service, to protect the President. He stated in an interview published December 23rd by *U.S. News & World Report*, "One of the things I

* The Commission's report says this was Mrs. R. A. Reid, a clerical supervisor.

don't understand is how he ever got out of that building. I wouldn't have let anyone out." And it was not the absence of police which was responsible for the escape of Oswald. On the contrary, as Baughman understands, they were already there and Oswald walked right through them. Baughman even marvels at the speed with which police had taken their positions at the exits. "Another thing I don't understand is how the police got up to that building so quickly, after the shots were fired," he says. Yet, according to the New York *Herald Tribune* of November 25th: "As Oswald left the building, he was again stopped by Dallas police. Oswald told them he worked in the building and was going down to see what was going on."

Oswald himself may be referred to as Accomplice Three. There is good reason to suspect that we may now identify Accomplice Four as the man responsible for letting Oswald leave the building. Any rookie cop on the police force would know better than to let men out of a building, after an assassination of the President of the United States. In this case there had been, moreover, a direct command from the police chief. Someone failed to do his duty. One is thus permitted to demand why he was never punished.

Oswald was by now provisionally free—thanks to Accomplice Four. And since the hare had been set loose, the hounds could follow. It is said to have been 12:33 when Oswald walked out of the murder building. The President's Commission says that by 12:45 police had ordered him to be arrested, sending out by radio an "all-points pickup."

How did the police contrive to solve this case so quickly? Here, as in the sequence of the bullets, there has been a change in the official story.

Until the report of the Commission had been published, the official explanation was that given by the man who would have had the job of prosecuting Oswald—Henry Wade—who said that Oswald first became a suspect when employees working in the building were assembled by their superintendent, Roy S. Truly, on command of the police, and one—and *only* one—was found at that time to be missing. "Every other employee was located," District Attorney Wade told *The New York Times* November 26th. "A description and name of him went out by police to look for him."

This is a curious reversal of position, it should be observed, before proceeding to analysis of all its implications. Until now, all Oswald had to do was to pronounce the magic words "I work here" and, as though he waved a wand, all gates were open to him. Although he had been the first man seen inside the building, the first officer who entered did not even bother to ask him for any information. This policeman was "somehow convinced that any sniper in the building must be a stranger and not an employee," *Time* deduced from his conduct. That does not account, however, for this officer's extraordinary failure to inquire if Oswald had observed suspicious characters within the building, or heard sounds which might assist him to locate the man for whom he was now searching. A few minutes later, when he had again been challenged by policemen, Oswald "told them he worked in the building and was going down to see what was going on." Apparently, these officers found that convincing. Suddenly, however, after Oswald left the building, the police decided that mere absence of employees from the area in which the murder was committed was itself suspicious—and sufficient evidence of possible complicity to send out an urgent radio appeal for the arrest of such an absent worker. It was not the fact that Roy S. Truly had seen Oswald in the lunchroom when he first rushed in the building that had caused suspicion. Truly made this very clear indeed, when quoted by the New York *Herald Tribune* of November 25th: "Mr. Truly said that he placed 'no significance' on Oswald's presence there 'until later when we found him missing and I reported it.' "

According to police reports, it was the radio description of Lee Oswald, following the roll call, that enabled Policeman Tippit in a scout car to recognize Oswald and to try to arrest him, which happened at 1:16, they contend. But there is evidence to show that this roll call did not take place prior to 1:16; it happened shortly after Tippit was reported murdered. Thus a radio alert based on the absence of Lee Oswald from the book depository could not have reached Tippit before he was shot.

Kent Biffle wrote the sequence of events preceding the discovery that Oswald was now missing in the Dallas *Morning News* on November 23rd: "The policeman and Truly continued their search. Oswald later failed to report at a 1:15 roll call of employees. Truly reported this to the police." In more detail, Biffle described how suspicion first fell on Lee Oswald. "An officer entered and told the lawmen that a policeman, J. D. Tippit, had just been killed. No details. An employee of the textbook firm walked up: 'I don't know if you're interested in this . . . but one of the fellows who works here is gone. Can't find him anywhere.' The police were interested. 'He's 23, about five-foot-nine and weighs around 150 pounds. I'd have to check the payroll records to be sure but I think he's been here a couple of months. His name is Lee Oswald.' "

This could not have taken place before 1:20, and accordingly investigators have discarded the first explanation that the order to arrest Lee Oswald came when it was known that he was missing. It is now asserted that Lee Oswald's name was never mentioned in police calls ordering arrest of the assassin; that he had not been suspected prior to the Tippit murder; and that radio descriptions at 12:45 and later were not based on information furnished by someone who knew Lee Oswald, but were "probably" supplied by an eyewitness in the street below him who looked up and caught a glimpse of someone in the sixth-floor window. It must be noted, at this point, that this is a remarkable confession for the President's Commission to have made: They are not certain, even now, who gave the order to arrest the suspect, and upon what information this policeman acted. One would think that this point could have been established by examination of police officials.

The eyewitness who is said to have identified Lee Oswald so precisely that Policeman Tippit, acting solely on this man's description, recognized him and attempted to arrest him, was Howard L. Brennan, who did not know Oswald at the time and was unable to identify him later, at Police Headquarters, the first time he saw him. After seeing Oswald's photograph on television, Brennan managed merely to affirm that Oswald bore a close resemblance to the man whom he had seen. It seems extraordinary, therefore, that he managed to provide policemen at the scene of the assassination with enough information to enable them to send out a quite accurate account of Oswald's height and weight. The feat is all the more remarkable when one considers that he based his estimate on the assumption that Oswald had been standing at the window, whereas the Commission says "most probably he was either sitting or kneeling. The half-open window, the arrangement of the boxes, and the angle of the shots virtually preclude a standing position." Yet the report says, "Brennan could have seen enough of the body of a kneeling or squatting person to estimate his height"!

It seems clear that if someone in the Police Department gave the order to arrest Lee Oswald, or a man with an identical description, prior to the Tippit murder, this policeman knew Oswald's role in the conspiracy already—and such knowledge was available to no one at that time except his fellow plotters. If that is the case, then the police official with this guilty knowledge is Accomplice Five, and of the ones that we have met so far, he is the most important.

Oswald seems to have been followed, as he left the building, by Accomplice Six, whose role was simply to survey him so that, at the proper moment, he could be arrested. This man, unlike his three predecessors, was probably not dressed in an official uniform, but, like the others, was in the Police Department. He was probably a plain-clothes detective. His existence is inferred from the rapidity with which police had access to the course of Oswald's flight across the city—information they possessed before the suspect had revealed it to them. They knew—or they said they knew—what Oswald said to other passengers aboard the bus; they knew where he got off, and why; they knew he walked a few blocks after that, and hailed a taxi. All this information was allegedly supplied by witnesses. The chain, however, was too rapid, and too perfect, and the witnesses were somehow not available when the reporters sought to interview them. Any cub reporter who has served his sentence in the press room of a metropolitan police department knows that, during any manhunt of this type, the switchboard at Police Headquarters is unable to keep up with all the tips that citizens phone in, of which the greater part are pure imagination—and to think that the police, relying solely on this type of information, managed promptly to distinguish information relative to Oswald from the mass of spurious, irrelevant material that was pouring in to them is to betray a total ignorance of problems which a manhunt poses. There was nothing to distinguish Oswald, at this time, from any person who was in the street. He was not wounded, and in all respects Lee Harvey Oswald was an extremely nondescript young man whom no one would be likely to remember. And it must be emphasized that he was trying, at this time, to be as inconspicuous as possible. It is, therefore, fantastic to assert that he would dare attract attention to himself by telling other passengers aboard the bus that Kennedy had just been shot, and *laughing*. This, however, is the story that District Attorney Wade related to reporters.

That the suspect, who was fleeing for his life, had laughed in public at the President's assassination seemed so clearly inconsistent with his perfect self-control in the canteen and with his subsequent denial of complicity that it is now conceded that it never happened. Nor could anyone aboard that bus, even if Oswald had behaved in the unlikely way attributed to him, have told police that he had later got into a cab, or managed to identify it, since by that time Oswald would have been out of sight.

There is some reason to suspect, however, that Accomplice Six encountered certain difficulties in pursuing Oswald. One suspects that he was reprimanded by the higher-placed conspirators for having been so obvious about it. Oswald seems to have observed that he was being followed, and he gave the taxi driver an address five blocks away from the cheap rooming house where he was living, probably with the desire to shake off his pursuer. He may even have attempted to evade him by appearing to go into an apartment house, then fleeing through the back door—or by any of the many subterfuges with which, thanks to Hollywood, we have all grown familiar. It may be assumed, however, that it didn't work, for even if the hare had managed to evade one hound, he would have had to reckon with a thousand others.

The suggestion has been made in Europe, notably by Serge Groussard in *l'Aurore* (a right-wing paper which may be regarded as the French equivalent of the Chicago *Tribune*), that Oswald's fellow plotters meant him to escape.

The whole plot, says Groussard, was carried out by gangsters with the aid of a corrupt policeman, who was meant to help Oswald get out of town by hiding him in his patrol car, double-crossed him and attempted to arrest him, and was consequently shot by Oswald. This is a compelling thesis, and is worth consideration. It will be examined in detail a little later.

J. D. Tippit, as reporters subsequently learned, had served ten years without promotion, though he is reported to have had a brother who became an officer in the Police Department. And he had a wife and three small children. Groussard thinks the lure of money was an irresistible temptation to him, and he speculates that gangsters had told Tippit that there was a member of the underworld who, on a certain date and hour, wanted to escape the city. Tippit, he believes, had no suspicion of the nature of the crime which this man planned to carry out; he probably believed the fugitive intended to hold up a bank, or to commit some robbery of that sort, and allowed himself to be persuaded to conceal the man in a police car until he had reached the next link in a relay system that would lead to safety. But when Tippit found out on his radio that Kennedy had just been murdered, he was struck by the suspicion that he had a rendezvous with the assassin. So, Groussard says, Tippit changed his mind. Impelled by patriotic indignation, or by mere desire to win himself a medal and promotion, he decided he would not help Oswald to escape but would arrest him, single-handed.

There are several persuasive arguments which tend to indicate that Tippit knew where Oswald had been and where he was going. One of these is that, despite the detailed nature of the physical description sent out by police, Lee Oswald would have been a hard man to recognize, except for someone who already knew him. He was average in height and weight; to complicate the problem, the description of his clothing was no longer valid. And to someone who did not know the assassin lived nearby, his presence would not be expected three miles from the assassination scene. The neighborhood where Tippit found him was, however, one in which two major actors in this drama had been living for the past few months. Jack Ruby and Lee Oswald, in a city as spread out as Dallas, both had homes in the same neighborhood. Each had moved there very recently. Until a short time before the President's assassination, Ruby had been living in a much more fashionable part of Dallas, just a few blocks from the home and office of former General Edwin A. Walker. Mark Lane told the President's Commission that he was informed that Ruby, Tippit and a man said to have been associated with the Birch Society had met in secret, one week prior to the assassination. It is worth consideration that when Justice Warren asked Jack Ruby if this meeting took place, Ruby was evasive—yet, as Dorothy Kilgallen pointed out, Warren made no attempt to get the witness to respond directly to the question. Although Ruby finally told Warren he did not know Tippit, Ruby's sister, Mrs. Eva Grant, had stated to the New York *Herald Tribune* on December 5th, "Jack called him buddy. . . . Jack knew him, and I knew him. He used to come into both the Vegas Club and the Carousel Club. . . . He was in and out of our place many times." And *Candide,* pro-Gaullist Paris weekly, quoted Mrs. Grant as saying that the ex-Chicago hoodlum and the Dallas law-enforcement officer were "like two brothers."

According to the Groussard thesis, Oswald was expecting Tippit. The policeman kept his rendezvous. There was no reason for the fugitive to be suspicious—and indeed, according to one witness, Oswald smiled at Tippit when he saw him, ambled over to the scout car, and they had an amicable conversation for almost a minute, Tippit staying in the car and Oswald standing in the street beside his rolled-down car window. Then, if ever, Oswald should have been off guard, and if he really had been planning to escape with Tippit's aid, it is not clear why he did not at once step into the police car. But the facts oppose the Groussard thesis, for after they had talked a moment, Tippit rolled up his car window as though he were planning to drive off. Oswald then resumed walking in the direction in which he had previously been going, apparently in the belief that Tippit would now drive away.

If the official version were correct, and Tippit had indeed reached the decision to arrest the suspect after his calm conversation with him, all his training would, at this time, have obliged him to pick up the radio beside him, give headquarters his exact location, and request assistance. There was nothing urgent in the situation that compelled him to leap from the car before he had accomplished that routine precaution. Witnesses agree that Oswald was not running from the car or threatening resistance.

The effect of lunging from the car and rushing after Oswald was precisely what the least experienced policeman on the force could have predicted. It provoked Lee Oswald to do what he had not yet been doing—to resist arrest. What Tippit did not know, however, is that Oswald would outdraw him.

Was it really Oswald? The attorney Mark Lane, author Joachim Joesten and, of course, Oswald himself, contest this. Their contention is based chiefly on deficiencies in identification of the killer by the chief eyewitness, Mrs. Helen Markham. Lane says Mrs. Markham told him that the man she saw kill Tippit was approximately thirty years old, bushy-haired and stocky, wearing a white cotton jacket. He points out that Oswald was considerably younger; had receding, rather short hair; was comparatively slender; and was wearing a tan plaid jacket. Mrs. Markham subsequently testified before the President's Commission and, according to Chief Justice Warren, she denied that she had ever talked to Lane. He said she furnished a description that could be interpreted to fit Lee Oswald. Warren thereupon announced that he had "every reason to doubt the truth-fulness" of Lane's reported conversation with the witness. Lane, in turn, retorted that he had a tape recording of it. Summoned for the second time before the President's Commission, he was asked by J. Lee Rankin, counsel for that body, "Did Mrs. Markham give permission to you or any-one to make that recording?" which Lane—properly, I think—regarded as a menace. But he offered, nonetheless, to let the President's Commission hear it, on condition that they would grant him immunity from prosecution for pos-session of it. It has frequently been played by Mr. Lane in public meetings, and it seems to be authentic. It is, further-more, confirmed by the account first published by the Dallas *Morning News:* "Witnesses to the shooting described a bushy-haired man about 30 as Tippit's slayer. They said he wore a white cotton jacket."

Doubt is raised, moreover, as to whether Oswald had the time, after he left the book depository at approximately 12:33, to make the three-mile trip afoot, by bus and finally by taxi to 500 North Beckley Avenue, where he got out and walked the last few blocks to his room; to enter the room, arm himself with his revolver and put on his jacket; and then to walk at least eight more blocks (depending on the route he took) to where the Tippit murder happened. The police have set the time at 1:16, but Lane says Mrs. Mark-ham told him it was slightly after 1:06. The latter time, if accurate, would almost certainly preclude the possibility that Oswald murdered Tippit.

I should be inclined to doubt the value of the testimony of this witness, and if Mrs. Markham's memory of the assas-sin's physical appearance is asserted to be so uncertain, it seems idle to rely upon her estimate of when the murder happened. Similar considerations prompt me to accept the paraffin test as authentic, and I am, indeed, the only one to do so! Those who think Oswald the lone assassin want us

134

to believe that portion of the laboratory report which states that Oswald's hands showed he had recently fired a revolver; at the same time, they reject as "inconclusive" the official finding which shows that he did not fire a rifle. Those who feel Oswald was innocent of both crimes have adopted the reverse position. They contend the absence of gunpowder on his cheeks is all-important, but its presence on his hands means nothing. Each side, I feel, yields to the temptation with which we are all afflicted to ignore the facts that are unpleasant. The test's implications are quite clear: They prove Lee Oswald innocent of the first crime, and guilty of the second.

I suggest that J. D. Tippit died, as stated by official sources, while attempting to obey the orders which he had received from his superiors in the Police Department. It is now too late to ask him what these orders may have been, and we can only speculate as to their nature. But since it is clear that the arrest of Oswald was not carried out by Tippit in accordance with approved police procedure, we must ask why it was not, and the hypothesis that follows is an effort to provide the answer.

The assignment of Policeman Tippit, it may be supposed, was to have been a vital one. He had been designated as the one to make the suspect's interception. The first act had gone according to the script. Oswald went to his room and got his gun, as he was meant to. He emerged, now armed and dangerous, and headed down the street toward a destination which had been assigned him. He believed he was escaping. If—as many writers have suggested —he was heading for Ruby's apartment, he was almost there now, and in this connection it is interesting to recall the story of Jim Lehrer in the Dallas *Times Herald* of December 20th that Ruby had made five reservations on a plane leaving for Mexico. But Oswald was not destined to reach any place of safety, for the moment he walked out the door it looks as though Detective Six, who had been waiting patiently for him to reappear, must have advised Patrolman Tippit, in a nearby scout car.

For the latter, it was to have been the opportunity to redeem a career which, until that time, had not been remarkably distinguished. Oswald now was armed, and Tippit would arrest him. During the arrest, the suspect would attempt to draw his gun and Tippit, with his life in peril, would be forced to shoot him. The sole suspect—the assassin—the pro-Castro, Communist fanatic—would be shot down in the street, and he would be forever silent. All the proof had been arranged—or would be soon arranged—to point suspicion at him. And the other members of the plot would all go free. There would be no one left to implicate them. The case could be closed officially, forever. . . .

Does this seem familiar to you? It should be. For what I am suggesting to you is that the assignment of Policeman Tippit was to be the role of Boston Corbett, the poor sergeant who shot Booth and afterwards went crazy. Though Booth's murder had been unpremeditated, it prevented the conviction on conspiracy to murder of the high Confederate officials—all because the one key witness, Booth, could never be produced in court against them.

That is how Accomplice Oswald was to have been silenced—not by any such crude method as was subsequently improvised. It seems inconceivable to me that the conspirators intended Oswald to be captured *living*, to deny his crime, and prompt a long investigation. That, I think, is the great logical defect in thinking the conspirators themselves killed Tippit, or that his death was completely unrelated. Nor has any motive for the Tippit slaying by the plotters been suggested, and they scarcely would have multiplied the risk of their detection by a publicly conducted murder of this sort; not only would it risk detection by eyewitnesses, but if Lee Oswald had already been arrested or could otherwise provide an alibi, it would be certain to expose them.

But Policeman Tippit bungled his assignment. There was no policeman with him, so that he could proceed to carry out his mission undisturbed. It was unthinkable to have sent any large detachment of policemen to effect the capture. Oswald might not have resisted them, might meekly have consented to his capture—and, at all costs, that risk was to be averted. The first honest officer to question him might learn the details of the whole conspiracy. A man who had not even fired the fatal shot would not have gone to the electric chair in silence, to protect his fellow plotters. Oswald had to be provoked to shoot it out. It had to look as though Policeman Tippit were compelled to shoot him. That is what he had been told: "Be sure to make it realistic. There are bound to be some witnesses. Don't just go up to him and shoot him." So Policeman Tippit followed orders. He dared Oswald, in effect, to draw his gun. And Oswald drew it. . . .

When Lee Oswald won the duel with his intended executioner, the minutely detailed timing of the play was interrupted, and for half an hour all the actors improvised their lines. The most confused, of course, was Oswald. He had been so close to safety, only to be thwarted by what must have seemed to him to be bad luck, and nothing more than that. He had no way of knowing that, if he had managed to attain the refuge to which he was heading, a policeman would no doubt have been there, waiting. To his credit, it must now be stated that Accomplice Oswald kept faith with his fellow plotters, even after they betrayed him. He did not lead the police to his imagined place of refuge, even though there is good reason to suppose that he had almost reached it. He assumed that anyone who shot down a policeman in the middle of the street, in downtown Dallas, in broad daylight, would soon have policemen all around him. So he turned his back on his own hopes of safety and ran in the opposite direction. Witnesses of Tippit's slaying differ. Most of them say that the killer was alone, but one says that another man ran after him. We may assume that all these witnesses are right, for Oswald was no doubt pursued, though at a distance, by Detective Six.

Detective Six was now in an embarrassing position. He had orders not to interfere with Oswald's capture and expected execution "while attempting to escape." He was, accordingly, too far away to intervene when Oswald unexpectedly shot Tippit. He may even have lost precious moments in reporting what had happened. It is possible he lost the trail, although this is not likely, since a short time later we have "witnesses" who saw the suspect run into a vacant lot, eject the spent shells and reload his pistol. After that, Accomplice Oswald—who must, by this time, have been amazed to find out that he had no visible pursuers—went into a motion picture theatre to conceal himself from the police who, he had every reason to believe, were looking for him in connection with the Tippit murder. There he stayed, until police came in and got him.

The police of Dallas who, needless to say, were not collectively involved in any plot even if a small handful of them had betrayed them, knew that one of their own men had just been murdered. They knew where the young man said to have fired the revolver was now hiding. They went into the Texas Theatre shortly before 2 o'clock, and they arrested Oswald. They had not the slightest notion, at that time, that Oswald was the President's assassin. The definitive assertion of this fact was made by Maurice McDonald, the policeman who made the arrest. He told Lloyd Shearer in an article appearing in *Parade,* "At the time I captured Oswald, I had no idea that he had killed the President of the United States. I was fairly sure, however, that he was the man who had killed Officer Tippit."

Officer McDonald did his duty. The police had their assassin—but they had a live one.

*   *   *

What was done about it is, of course, no secret. But before Jack Ruby came into the picture, there were two days of suspense for all those implicated in the plot. Would Oswald talk? The greatest danger was in the beginning. Some way had to be discovered that would minimize this possibility. Oswald was, accordingly, not charged at first with being an accomplice to the President's assassination. The police began to question him exclusively about the Tippit murder. All the while the press was being told the whole assassination had been planned and executed by one man—the man who had just been arrested—the police were questioning the prisoner about another case entirely. For as long as they were able to maintain the prisoner in isolation, they permitted him to think that he was just a suspect in the murder of which he alone was guilty.

This fact was made clear by the Dallas *Morning News* of November 23rd: "Shortly after midnight, Curry and Wade held a formal press conference announcing the filing of charges in the President's murder. Oswald later was brought into the crowded police squad room. In response to reporters' questions, the defendant said he had requested counsel. He said the 'judge gave me a hearing that was very short and sweet.' When asked if he killed the President, Oswald replied: 'I have not been told that I have been charged with the murder of the President.' Wade confirmed that the man had not been advised of charges in

139

connection with the President's slaying. But he had been told of his charges in the death of the patrolman."

It must, from that moment, have become apparent to him that his friends had double-crossed him, and each hour that he lived thereafter, the conspirators whom he was able to identify knew that their own lives were increasingly in danger. Oswald, by this time, was openly insisting on his right to see a lawyer. He made this demand before reporters. Yet, for two days of persistent questioning, this right—which is assured to any man under the Constitution—was relentlessly denied him. It would not be possible to keep this up much longer. And if Oswald saw a lawyer, the first question he would ask would be, "What chance have I to get off with a prison term, instead of the electric chair, if I confess and name my fellow plotters?" The same question Lloyd had asked in 1865 after the death of Lincoln—and the tavern keeper who had helped Mrs. Surratt to furnish Booth with weapons, and was probably as guilty as the others who were sentenced to be hung or jailed for life, escaped unpunished, simply by becoming an informer.

Oswald never asked that question, thanks to the prompt intervention of Jack Ruby, who declared, when he had been arrested, "I couldn't forget how Jackie had suffered, and that Caroline and John wouldn't have a daddy any more." These fine sentiments, however, may be disregarded, since the counsel for Jack Ruby say that, at that moment, he was crazy.

Prosecutor Henry Wade proved, on the other hand, to the apparent satisfaction of a Dallas jury that Jack Ruby was a sane man when he killed Lee Oswald. But he offered no convincing reason for the crime's premeditation. Was it merely for publicity and glory? The electric chair seems an expensive price for advertising. Did he have a patriotic reason? One of Ruby's ex-associates says that the only

Presidents in whom Jack Ruby ever showed much interest were those whose pictures he collected on dollar bills.

A more realistic explanation was provided by Detective "Bill X" of the Dallas police in an interview with J.-P. Renard of *Paris-Presse:*

Q. Tell me about Ruby.

A. You know as much about him as I do.

Q. Was he a police informer?

A. Yes, in his spare time.

Q. Why did you let him come into Police Headquarters when Oswald was going to be transferred?

A. We were used to seeing him there often. We used to play dominoes and cards with him. Besides, there were about sixty people there that day, reporters, cameramen, technicians, F.B.I. men. One more or less didn't matter.

Q. Nevertheless, didn't his presence there even surprise you?

A. No, he belonged there—let me put it that way. . . .

Q. Why, in your opinion, did he kill Oswald?

A. He undoubtedly had his reasons.

Q. By patriotism, as he claimed?

A. That all depends on what you call patriotism. Patriotism might mean a lot of things. Saving your own skin, for instance.

Q. By risking the electric chair?

A. You gamble, double or nothing. With a good lawyer, you can get off.

As any gambler knows, the man who gambles all he has, hoping to break even, has so much at stake that he cannot stop playing. It appears Jack Ruby was in that position. He was not the only one, however. There appear to have been men in the Police Department who had just as much to lose as he did. It would not be too surprising if this group had merged, for mutual protection.

A strong hint of this was given in the testimony at the Ruby trial. It was argued, on behalf of Ruby, that he could not have killed Oswald with premeditation since he would have needed the cooperation of police in order to have carried out his murder. By this, Ruby's lawyer was not referring simply to the fact that Ruby, as already stated, was permitted entrance to a building from which all outsiders were excluded during Oswald's transfer. He made the much more important point that no one but police—or those in whom police confided—could have known that Oswald would still be there at the time that Ruby reached the prison. It had been announced that Oswald would be moved from the Dallas city jail to a nearby jail operated by Dallas County at 10 A.M. That was the time, therefore, that the general public and the press expected the transfer to take place. But, as the lawyer demonstrated, Ruby was still miles away at that time. He did not walk into the Dallas city jail until 11:19. Oswald was put on the elevator by the police only a moment later, and brought, handcuffed, to the exact spot where Jack Ruby was now standing. The fatal shot was fired at 11:21, precisely two minutes after Ruby came into the building. A policeman, Detective Thomas McMillon, testified Jack Ruby told him after he shot Oswald, "You all won't believe this, but I didn't have this planned. I couldn't have timed it so perfect. I got there just when Oswald was coming out." And Ruby added, "Someone had to do it. You guys couldn't. You didn't think I was going to let him get away with it, did you?"

*   *   *

"You guys" had an ambulance beside the jail door, waiting, just in case something should happen to Lee Harvey Oswald as he left his cell under police protection. The official pessimism proved well-founded, and because of this extraordinary foresight Oswald was, indeed, rushed to the hospital in record time—the same hospital where the President had died.

Did the two men know each other? That is certainly suggested by the phrasing of Jack Ruby's statement, "You didn't think I was going to let him get away with it, did you?" It has never been part of the Ruby system of defense that he killed Oswald, fearing that a jury might acquit the President's accused assassin; he has, on the contrary, declared that waiting for the Oswald trial would have been "useless" because it was certain that he would be convicted and there was no use subjecting Mrs. Kennedy to the ordeal of testifying. Ruby claimed that he was merely speeding the inevitable execution of a sentence which was not in doubt. Accordingly, by his own testimony, Ruby never for a moment thought that Oswald had a chance to "get away with" Kennedy's assassination. Thus his cryptic statement must be subject to a different interpretation. It seems clearly to refer to Tippit's murder. Here, again, however, there is nothing which would indicate that Ruby feared Oswald would not be executed for it. Thus the "crime" which only Ruby could avenge, which "someone had to do," which "you guys couldn't"—that must be some personal vendetta, in which Ruby felt that he could count on the benevolent neutrality of the police. The thing he feared Oswald might "get away with" cannot have been just the murder; it sounds rather like the language of a man who feels another one has double-crossed him, by attempting to evade the role for which he had been destined.

Ruby and Lee Oswald were not only neighbors in the Dallas section where they both were living, and to which they had both moved within a short time of each other— they were also neighbors in the postal boxes they had rented. This would, no doubt, have been written off as

143

mere coincidence if, from the very outset, there had not been witnesses who swore that they had seen the two together. Thus, Jean-Pierre Renard wrote on November 27th in *Paris-Presse:* "The second conclusion of the F.B.I., which has started a fresh investigation, is that Jack Ruby, Oswald's murderer, and Oswald himself had been in contact only a few days before the assassination. 'We are not yet absolutely certain of this,' Dallas Mayor Cabell informed me a few hours ago, 'but there are strong indications that it is true. We are checking every possibility. That's one of them. In fact, it's the most important lead we have.' " Renard continued, "The F.B.I. investigation has established another essential point: Oswald and Ruby met each other prior to the assassination. The principal witness to this effect is a 22-year-old ventriloquist, Bill de Mar, whose real name is Bill Crowe, and who was performing at the Carousel, one of Ruby's night clubs. He says he saw Oswald and Ruby talking over a glass of whisky 'eight or nine days' before the assassination. Since filing his deposition, whose existence is confirmed by the Dallas police, Bill de Mar has disappeared from the city. It appears that he has been put under the protection of the F.B.I., a fact which emphasizes the importance of his statement."

One of the chief subjects of newspaper speculation, in the weeks before the Ruby trial, was whether testimony of De Mar and other witnesses—the New York *Herald Tribune* said there were at least ten—would be offered to the jury by the prosecutor, to establish that Jack Ruby knew the man he murdered. The defense, of course, hoped to exclude them, since if the defendant could be shown to have had prior contact with his victim, this would tend to prove premeditation on the part of Ruby. But the prosecution did not want them, either. The official version now excluded any link between the first crime and the second. So there was a gentleman's agreement, which was not confined to Wade

144

and Belli. It included Washington's participation. This is how it happened, as revealed by Dorothy Kilgallen in the Hearst press, February 23rd:

On January 9th, defense attorney Joe Tonahill wrote F.B.I. Director Hoover, asking him to furnish the defense with "all the reports and minutes and evidence in possession of the Johnson-Warren commission." On January 28th, Assistant Attorney General Herbert J. Miller replied that the F.B.I. would be instructed to turn over to Ruby's counsel the names and addresses of everyone they knew who had ever known Jack Ruby or related to the F.B.I. incidents which might be useful in the preparation of the case for the defense. Only one condition was attached, however. Miller said that "information concerning Oswald's assassination of the President will not be available as it does not appear relevant." Miss Kilgallen commented, "Perhaps it is dramatizing to say there is an Orwellian note in that line. But it does make you think." And she concluded that "the unprecedented alliance between Ruby's lawyers and the Department of Justice" suggested "that Washington knows or suspects something about Lee Harvey Oswald that it does not want Dallas and the rest of the world to know or suspect. . . . Oswald has passed on to the mysterious realm of 'classified' persons whose whole story is known to only a few Government agents."

The Ruby trial thus dragged to its conclusion March 14th without an opportunity to hear at least ten men and women testify in court, and under cross-examination, that Lee Oswald and Jack Ruby knew each other. Prosecutor Henry Wade decided that he did not need them, to prove the defendant guilty of premeditation. And on April 11th, a reporter for the *National Enquirer* found Bill de Mar, Jack Ruby's former employee, in a nightclub in Indiana. De Mar had not changed his view that Oswald had been in the Carousel with Ruby, but he seemed to be resigned now

145

to the fact that no one would believe him. "I gave the F.B.I. a statement about seeing Oswald in the club and that was it," he stated. "I told them the same thing I'm telling you. I signed it and have heard nothing more about the incident to this day."

There was a great wave of indignation in the press, after the fight in which the "good guy," Sonny Liston, was defeated by the "villain," Cassius Clay. Reporters hinted that "the fix was in" and protest was expressed that a world heavyweight crown could have changed hands by a mutual agreement of the two contending parties, who would settle their accounts in a return match which would, this time, be decided on the merits of the two contenders' fists. But there were few protesting voices raised when Henry Wade's hand was raised as the victor over the defense attorney, Belli, in a trial which was designed to throw some light upon the way in which the Presidency of the United States had changed hands. To me, as a reporter for *l'Express*, both lawyers were victorious in this fight. Belli had won all the legal points; he had more than enough of them to find at least one legal error which an appeals court would eventually rule to be reversible. He had, accordingly, succeeded in the job that counted—keeping Jack Ruby from the electric chair. But Henry Wade had been content to watch Belli pile legal point on legal point; he was not interested in the way the case would be decided, after it left Dallas—he was solely interested in the verdict of the jury. His approach was, therefore, psychological, not legal. Henry Wade gets what he wants, in Dallas. Of the 24 preceding cases in which he had asked for the death sentence, 23 received it. And accordingly, on March 5th, nine days prior to the verdict of the jury, I cabled my editors as follows: "Contrary to general opinion, Ruby risks death sentence. Belli winning all the technical points. Wade's psychology is winning jury." *L'Express* subsequently photographed this cable for its readers.

Ruby did not, at that time, appear too worried. He seemed confident that his friends would protect him. After all, as he had told his sister, on the night he was arrested for the Oswald murder, "I've got a lot of friends. I know lots of the police and the F.B.I. men. Don't you worry; they'll treat me all right."

*   *   *

There were many things in Texas that the foreign newsmen noticed. That in Dallas there are more men murdered each year than in all of England. That it is a city where a man can buy a lethal weapon with the same ease that a European buys a flashlight.

But the thing that struck the European correspondents most was the report that the police and an ex-hoodlum from Chicago had been playing dominoes together at Police Headquarters. That is something that is just not done in Europe. Oh, of course they have their business relations in Pigalle, for instance, and the girls in the Rue St. Denis all pay their taxes to the members of the vice squad, one way or another. But the French police officials do not play "421" with the white slavers to see who is buying the aperitifs. A dim view would be taken of a British bobby who was seen too often in the local pub, sipping his beer and throwing darts with a train robber.

Certain European journalists deduced from this that Dallas was a city run by gangsters, and that Kennedy was murdered by the Mafia. To which Americans replied with indignation or derision. Both sides were a little hasty in announcing their conclusions. Each saw what the other didn't.

For an observer in a foreign land, the elements which

are the most conspicuous are those which are most strange, and he is tempted to confuse mere strangeness with significance.

A stranger sleeping in an unfamiliar house may plausibly erect, from creaking steps and the low whistling of the wind, a series of hypotheses ranging from ghosts to burglars, but the person who has lived there, entering a room, will generally find the element that is discordant—if he tries to find it.

On the other hand, the owner of that house may climb the stairway to his room each night, no longer noticing the broken strip of railing which he has been meaning to repair for years—and then, one day, may stumble and be forced to lean upon it, and go plunging to his death. A stranger, once he had observed the danger, would have been more careful.

The United States is full of broken railings which we have been meaning to repair, but we have grown accustomed to them. One of these is that, in many cities, members of the underworld and those who operate upon its fringes are in friendly contact with police and they co-operate with one another. This is not confined to Dallas. Senator Kefauver's probe of criminal activities revealed that in New York, for instance, the police, the judges, the municipal officials and the gangsters had been sharing their illicit profits. This condition, Senator Kefauver said in 1951, was general, and his committee blamed it partly on corruption of local police chiefs and district attorneys. Part of the responsibility was placed, however, on the F.B.I. and other federal investigators, since the syndicate controlling local gangs was in the habit, it was found, of shifting its employees from one city to another, and from state to state.

During the 1930's, Senator La Follette had conducted a prolonged investigation of the use by large employers of "detectives" and strikebreakers who had been recruited from the underworld, whose function was to beat and, in some cases, murder labor organizers—yet they worked with the municipal police and state militia to combat formation of the labor unions. If organized crime has attained its present dimensions, it is thus because respectable citizens use criminals to carry out objectives beneficial to themselves, on which they do not wish to soil their hands. Though such objectives generally are of economic origin, they are political in their expression and, in 1939, Director of the F.B.I. J. Edgar Hoover stated that the files on all the major criminals sought by the F.B.I. revealed these criminals to have been under the protection of some politician. The constant contact of the underworld with businessmen and politicians has enabled criminals to share, in an increasing measure, the respectability of those they deal with. Frequently, the public does not even recognize these men as "gangsters," since they are engaged in perfectly legitimate activities which furnish a large portion of their income. This new trend is pointed out by C. Wright Mills in his book *The Power Elite:*

> Put bluntly, crime, if organized on a proper businesslike basis, pays. American gangsters, we now know, are the syndicated personnel of nationwide businesses, having syndicated connections with one another and with local public authorities. But more important than the fact that illegal businesses are now well-organized industries is the fact that the "hoods" of the twenties have in the forties and fifties become businessmen who own hotels and distilleries, resorts and trucking companies. Among such members of the fraternity of success, to have a police record means merely that you did not know the right people.

Every citizen of the United States knows privately within him that if you "know" someone at Police Headquarters, you can "fix" a parking ticket; that if you know someone even higher, you can rape a woman, beating her until she is almost unconscious, and police will tell her she seduced you—but not many people will admit that if you know somebody high enough, it is quite literally possible to get away with murder. Still less will the average American concede that such a murder could have taken place in a police headquarters with complicity of some of the police—that is to say, not many *white* Americans are willing to admit that.

But complicity of the police with Ruby seemed so evident to people of all countries, all political opinions, outside the United States that any possibility that the official explanation of the President's assassination might have been accepted was, thereafter, shattered.

This reaction was most eloquently stated by Raymond Cartier, one of France's most influential journalists and a staunch conservative, writing in *Paris-Match,* the French equivalent of *Life:*

> There exists a remarkable contrast between America and Europe, in regard to the assassination of President John F. Kennedy [he wrote in late December]. In America, it is scarcely an exaggeration to declare that the affair is on its way to being classified and filed. . . . The chance encounter of an anarchist and an exhibitionist, of a depressive paranoid and one who had grown manic—that is essentially the explanation being given for the tragedy of Dallas. America accepts this conclusion. Europe, almost in its totality, rejects it. Europeans are convinced the Dallas drama hides a mystery which, if uncovered, would dishonor the United States and shake it to its foundations. So it is better to hide it. Europe might perhaps be induced to believe the explanation of the solitary individual killing the President of the United States upon the street, as not even a dog is killed. But the explanation of the police informer, the proprietor of a house of ill repute, the pimp, the professional gangster killing the President's assassin out of patriotic indignation— Europe does not believe it for a moment. Europe finds the

story laughable. It throws upon the hitherto plausible explanation of a solitary Oswald an overwhelming doubt. It brings to view such abysses, in the crime of Dallas, that the eye recoils before them. It justifies suspicion of a deliberate and desperate concealment, carried out by all the organs of authority in the American nation. . . .

Le Figaro, the leading French conservative newspaper, an equivalent of the New York *Herald Tribune,* on November 28th charged investigators of the Dallas crime with "contradictions, obscurities, intentional omissions, deliberate lies." *Le Monde,* which corresponds to *The New York Times* and is, perhaps, the most objective paper in the world, declared November 27th that there were only two likely explanations for the "contradictions" the authorities in Dallas had been making. One was that, to hide their guilt for their inadequate security precautions, they had picked up the first suspect they could find and then selected evidence that seemed to fit him. The alternative was that they "considered it advisable to choose a 'suspect' in advance, who could be charged with full responsibility not only for the murder of President Kennedy but also that of the police officer, while at the same time shielding the real criminal."

Lest it be thought that such suspicions were exclusively the product of the Latin mind, it would be relevant to cite the first reaction of the head of India's Swatantra Party, Chakravarti Rajagopalachari, whom *Time* describes as "strongly pro-American." He said he thought that Oswald had been killed to "prevent the exposure of the conspiracy behind the crime," and he suggested "there may be big money behind the plot." Even the most respected of the London papers, noted for their understatement, voiced suspicion. A review of the British edition of this book in the *Economist* expressed it this way: "The present record does contain apparent discrepancies," while the London

Times said, "There *are* missing links." In Ireland, Donald Carroll, a reporter for the Irish Press who had been born and lived for 20 years in Dallas, culminated five long articles in July, 1964, with this conclusion: The official story, which he calls the "Authorized Version," is "a weird mosaic of contradictions, reversals and fabrications," and "the suspicion is irresistible that one of the conspirators might well be wearing, or might have worn, a police uniform."

It is worth recalling that the first, spontaneous reaction of Americans was not much different from that of the majority of people in these other countries. Most Americans believed in the beginning that Jack Ruby knew Lee Oswald. Even after a long press campaign asserting this belief to be unfounded, 40 percent of the United States still believed it and in Dallas, among those I talked to, the percentage was much higher, though in Washington newspapermen recoiled in horror at the mere suggestion. Ruby makes a singularly unconvincing agent of the Kremlin and, if the suspicion was correct that he killed his accomplice to insure his silence, most Americans found it unlikely that it was a left-wing plot. The first Gallup poll revealed that only 1 percent thought Oswald acted as the agent of a Communist conspiracy; 29 percent thought no one helped him in the President's assassination; 52 percent believed he represented an extreme right-wing group, gangsters, or some "unknown" force; the others had, presumably, not read the papers. Many of the leading magazines, newspapers, and diverse groups active in manipulating popular opinion still persisted in accepting the first thesis that the Communists ought, somehow, to be blamed—and the John Birch Society took full-page ads in *The New York Times* and in other papers to proclaim this viewpoint. But a full year after the assassination, few Americans could say with real conviction that they were quite certain they now knew the truth about what happened.

The prevailing feeling was described May 27th by New York *World Telegram & Sun* reporter Kenneth L. Dixon, who wrote following a six-week trip around the country, "I did not encounter one single person who believed he or she had been told the whole truth. . . . Most of those questioned indicated a complete lack of faith in the official reports on the case. . . . Offhand, I cannot recall any time, in peace or war, when this was such a universal reaction."

There is, then, a vague but very prevalent suspicion that some element in the official story does not quite ring true, and yet most people cannot put their finger on it. This is an example of that too-familiar room in which the sole discordant element should be apparent to the man who lives there.

Europeans saw the broken railing which Americans refused to see—the link between police and Ruby. It was strange to them that this link, which appears to them to be so glaring, did not cause more indignation in America—indeed, appeared almost to pass unnoticed.

But there is another clue which we shall need, if we are ever to resolve the mystery of Dallas. It is of a nature which would not attract attention by an Englishman or Frenchman, yet it is essential to our understanding of the principal enigma of this case—Lee Oswald.

It is not unusual in France, for instance, for a Communist to be employed in a top scientific post by the De Gaulle administration, and Professor J. D. Bernal, known to be a spokesman for that party, held a major wartime post in Britain. The United States, however, in the decade between the decline of Senator McCarthy and the rise of the Goldwater movement, never relaxed the severe curtailment of employment opportunities for an acknowledged Leftist. Communists, or persons who overtly act as though they were in sympathy with Communist objectives, could not get a job in 1963 with any agency of government or any private employer who provided government supplies. This has been carefully defined by law, where federal suppliers are concerned; it is a matter of accepted policy, upon the state and local level.

It extends to the most humble worker, not just to those who are in the "sensitive" positions. Many states and cities have, in fact, passed laws requiring their employees to take "loyalty oaths" to the United States. In California, for example, fourteen-year-old Stephen Sublett got in trouble in December, 1963, with the Los Angeles authorities when he refused to sign this oath. The job he sought was that of a dishwasher in the cafeteria of the school he attended; Stephen's pay was to consist of a free lunch each time he washed the dishes, and the school officials advised his parents that if Stephen would not promise not to overthrow the government, they would be forced to fire him. California is relatively liberal on matters like this in comparison to Texas, where the penaltes for all pro-Communist activity are not confined to state employees, but extend to all inhabitants of Texas.

In 1954, the Governor of Texas, Allan Shivers, asked the legislature of that state to pass a law to punish persons who might, in the future, undertake pro-Communist activities in Texas, although he admitted that at that time there were so few radicals in Texas "that it can't be called a problem." He felt very strongly that mere membership, apart from any overt action, was sufficient to require the penalty that he demanded: death. The legislators felt this might be slightly in excess of any penalty permitted by the U. S. Constitution and reduced it to a maximum of $20,000 fine and 20 years in prison.

It would be a brave man, therefore, who would go into the state of Texas and proclaim himself to be a Marxist, which is what Lee Oswald did—a brave man, and a most imprudent one, *unless he had somebody to protect him.* And of all the cities in the state of Texas, the last place a radical would go to, looking for a job, was Dallas, *unless he already had a job.*

That is the clue for which we have been looking: Oswald was not, at this time, what he professed to be—a Marxist—and there is good reason to suppose he never was.

According to his mother, Oswald's interest in Communism started from the time he entered the Marine Corps, at the age of seventeen. Oswald himself once stated that he started reading Marxist books before this, but the circumstances under which he made this statement, and the way in which Oswald expressed it, cast considerable doubt upon its accuracy. There have been no witnesses who can remember him engaging in pro-Communist activity as a schoolboy; yet a short time after he had volunteered for the Marines, his fellow servicemen report that he began to study Russian and receive newspapers from the Soviet Union. Even during World War II, when the U.S.S.R. was an ally, this would have been imprudent, for known Communists were generally put in special units where they could be watched, and where no matter which concerned a military secret would come to their attention. But when Oswald joined the service in October, 1956, the anti-Communist indoctrination of U. S. Marines was such that open Marxists would, presumably, have been court-martialed. As for any private who would dare defend a Marxist thesis in debates with his lieutenant, in the presence of his fellow soldiers, the exploit defies belief—yet this was stated by an ex-Marine who knew him, Nelson Delgado, in testimony to the President's Commission. He said it happened often, and that Oswald seemed to take great pleasure in it, yet was never punished. And not only this—he was thereafter given an assignment in a highly classified branch of the

service which, it can be reasonably assumed, required security clearance considerably more stringent than that
needed by an ordinary Marine. Oswald's former lieutenant,
John E. Donovan, was interviewed in Washington by the
Associated Press on December 4th. He said that when Lee
Oswald subsequently went to Russia and announced he
wanted to give up his citizenship, "that compromised all
our secret radio frequencies, call signs and authentication
codes. He knew the location of every unit on the West
Coast and the radar capability of every installation. We had
to spend thousands of man-hours changing everything."
One finds it very difficult to think that a Marine to whom
such vital information was entrusted could conduct himself as though he were a prospective traitor, make no effort
to conceal it, and remain unchallenged—unless he was, at
that time, pursuing training which had the approval of
someone above him. The deciding argument on this point,
which to my mind is irrefutable, is the fact that when
Oswald returned to the United States after his stay in
Russia, he was never prosecuted for the serious offense of
having compromised the secret codes of the Marine Corps,
with the ensuing loss of "thousands of man-hours" that this
cost the servicemen he left behind him.

Oswald had applied for a release from the Marine Corps,
after three years' service, to assist his mother, who was sick
at that time. The request was granted, but when Oswald
got home he informed his mother that he had a job which
would require him to leave home at once. "I'll see a lot and
it's good work," he told her. On October 13, 1959, Oswald
arrived in Moscow where, on October 31st, he told the U. S.
Embassy in Moscow that he wished to stay in Russia and
become a citizen of the U.S.S.R. He was interviewed by
several reporters, notably by Aline Mosby, to whom he asserted he had been a Marxist since the age of fifteen, when
"we moved to North Dakota and I discovered one book in

the library, *Das Kapital.*" The trouble with this story is, according to his mother, that the Oswald family had never lived in North Dakota.

Though the Soviets, on some occasions, have accepted applications from Americans who sought to acquire citizenship in their country, they rejected Oswald's bid. He soon became aware they did not trust him, that his mission was a failure. He is said, then, to have made a suicide attempt, resulting in the psychiatric test which normally is given after such an incident. The test was negative, however; Oswald was not found to be insane and they released him, giving him a minor job in Minsk which bored him; this was certainly not what he had expected when he told his mother, "I'll see a lot and it's good work." His mother wrote him that perhaps she'd like to come and live in Russia, too; he wrote back, "I don't recommend it." He asked her to send him an extremely strange list of material to read, for one whose tastes in the Marines had been so oriented toward ideology: Western stories and science fiction. He also asked for *Time* or *Newsweek* magazine, and for *1984* by anti-Soviet author George Orwell, whom he mistakenly identified with H. G. Wells. At last he gave up completely, and asked the U. S. Embassy to send him home, writing to former Secretary of the Navy Connally that "the U. S. Government has no charges or complaints against me. . . . I have and have always had the full sanction of the U. S. Embassy in Moscow." He also wrote his mother he was coming home, and added he could not go there directly because he "had to spend a day or two in Washington." He asked for, and received, a loan to finance his return, together with his wife and child; this loan of $435.71 was paid back by Lee Oswald in about seven months, although it seems incredible that he had saved this money from his meager income.

In June, 1962, a short time after his return, Oswald went

to Pauline Bates, a Fort Worth, Texas, public stenographer. He had a manuscript that he had written, dealing with the hardships he said he experienced in Russia, and for three days she typed notes for a book he said he was planning to submit for publication. In this book, Miss Bates said, he was violently hostile to the Russians. He wrote that their living standards were deplorable, that families were crowded into one room, that the Communists were always listening with hidden microphones and trying to hear his conversation. He condemned not only Russia but the principles of Communism. He did not tell Miss Bates he had gone there with pro-Communist convictions but was disillusioned. He implied instead that he had really been a secret agent. "When the State Department granted my visa," Oswald told her, "they stipulated they could not stand behind me in any way." But Oswald hinted strongly that he was a kind of free-lance spy, without government assistance but with government approval.

One year later, on June 24, 1963, Lee Oswald asked the State Department for a passport to go back to the same country which, he told Miss Bates, he hated. How he planned to find the money for this trip is, once again, a mystery; he had no savings at the time, his wife was pregnant with their second child, and he was only intermittently employed in low-paid jobs. But how Lee Oswald ever could have been so optimistic as to think that he would be allowed a passport is still more mysterious. The form which any ordinary citizen fills out, applying for a passport, states, "I have not . . . taken an oath or made an affirmation or other formal declaration of allegiance to a foreign state . . . made a formal renunciation of nationality either in the United States or before a diplomatic or consular officer of the United States in a foreign state; ever sought or claimed the benefits of the nationality of any foreign state. . . ." As has been indicated, Oswald had appeared October 31, 1959, before the vice-consul of the United States in Moscow and turned in his passport, with the statement that he no longer wished U. S. nationality; on November 2nd, he signed a declaration which said, "I affirm my allegiance to the Soviet Socialist Republic." At the bottom of the U. S. passport application there is the provision: "If any of the above-mentioned acts or conditions have been performed by or apply to the applicant . . . a supplementary explanatory statement under oath (or affirmation) by the person to whom the portion is applicable should be attached and made a part of this application."

One would have assumed that such a statement would have been minutely studied, but in Oswald's case the application was not only granted—*it arrived the next day!*

It has been asserted by the President's Commission that Lee Oswald was entitled to receive his passport because his request to change his nationality had not been processed by the U. S. Embassy in Moscow. "Oswald did not execute the proper forms, he did not sign his letter of October 31 or November 3, 1959, in the presence of a consular official, and neither letter was signed by such an official," the report says. "Although Lee Harvey Oswald wrote that his allegiance was to the Soviet Union, there is no indication that he had ever actually taken an oath or declaration," this extraordinary document continues. Yet, as has been shown, "formal renunciation of nationality" is not the only basis for denial of a passport. It was quite sufficient that he "sought or claimed the benefits of the nationality of any foreign state," and whether Oswald managed to complete the necessary forms or not, there cannot be the slightest doubt that this is what he "sought." Thus, while conceivably he was entitled to receive his former passport to effect repatriation, he could not have been expected to receive one in June, 1963, without a serious investigation of his new intentions.

Someone in the State Department seems to have made a notation against Oswald's name on the list of 25 applications they received June 24, 1963. The President's Commission is quite clear about this; it says that beside his name someone wrote "No" in red pencil. The Commission says that it has been informed, however, that the red notation did not mean someone had disapproved the Oswald application. The two letters, "N" and "O," did not mean "No" —they meant New Orleans, where Lee Oswald lived at that time!

On September 26th, Lee Oswald, armed with his new passport, went to Mexico to use it. Here again, the question that arises is: Where did he get the money? In discussing this trip, as well as the contemplated Russian voyage, Chief Justice Warren told reporters on February 5th, "The trips may have security aspects, and if they do, we could not release the security matters at the time of our report." He added that there were some aspects of the case that might not be revealed "within your lifetime." Oswald is reported to have asked the Cuban consulate in Mexico City to give him a transit visa for passage through Havana on his way to Russia. It may be remarked at this point that the penalty he risked was a five-year jail sentence and $5,000 fine, *unless he had the State Department's permission to enter Cuba.* But the Cuban consulate official told him he would have to wait for the request to be approved. Oswald walked out and slammed the door. He then went to the office of the Soviet consul general, where he introduced himself as a militant Communist and asked for a visa to enter Russia. The consul told him there would be a long investigation, a delay of four months, and approval was not certain. Once more, Oswald stalked out in abusive indignation. He returned to Texas, empty-handed, on October 3rd.

The Federal authorities not only were remarkably informed on the details of Oswald's trip to Mexico—they knew what food he ate, the problems he encountered when endeavoring to speak in Spanish, and they even knew what conversation Oswald had *inside the Cuban consulate*—but, most important, they knew Oswald planned to make the trip before he made it. A U.P.I. dispatch dated November 25th quotes customs officer William M. Kline at Laredo, Texas, as declaring that "a federal agency in Washington" asked to be notified when Oswald crossed the border. If Lee Oswald was, in fact, the lone assassin and confided his plans to nobody, it seems clear that the sole source of advance information on the trip, plus details of what Oswald told the Cubans, must have been the only person capable of giving them this information. That would be Lee Oswald.

Oswald does not seem to have been one of the C.I.A.'s more successful agents; on the other hand, he does not seem to have been one of their more highly paid ones either. One assumes that, had the Russians given him his visa, he would somewhere have obtained the money to finance the trip, and while in the U.S.S.R. he would have gone to Minsk, where he had formerly been working. Minsk, it happens, is a city which intrigues U. S. intelligence. In this connection, it is interesting to observe that in his U. S. passport application in June, 1963, he was required to state his occupation. Oswald wrote "photographer."

Oswald had a mediocre education, but the test he took when he went into the Marine Corps rated him above the average in his intelligence and would have qualified him for selection as a candidate for higher training, had he possessed the necessary formal education. Oswald was ambitious and adventurous by nature. After his return from Russia, there was just one way in which he could have hoped to rise above the life to which he otherwise was doomed, the long succession of stock clerk jobs for which he seemed fated. The profession for which he was now uniquely qualified was that of double agent. He had, from the age of seventeen, identified himself in public as a Marxist. This, he seems to have believed, would open doors to him in the U.S.S.R. and Cuba. The same logic evidently led him to conclude that, with his background, he could readily establish contact with left-wing groups in America. In April, 1963, *for the first time in Oswald's life,* he did this. For a man alleged to have been dedicated to the Communist world revolution, it seems curious that Oswald never previously had felt the need to talk to other citizens of the United States who shared this feeling.

Oswald had been seeing other people since his return from Russia, but there is no indication that among these friends were any persons of left-wing persuasion. One important clue, which Southerners will most appreciate, is that no Negroes ever were reported to have visited his home. Oswald's ostensible ideological affiliation would have made such social contact a political and moral obligation. One of his ex-landladies, Mrs. F. M. Tobias, told a private investigator with whom I have been in contact that the man he saw most often was called "George."

This "George" has subsequently been identified by the administrative aide of one of Dallas' most noted right-wing leaders (who did not say where he got the information) as the business associate of a California oil firm, and the husband of a Philadelphia oilman's daughter; he was said to have spent some time in Haiti, Guatemala and Cuba "for the U. S. Government."

Oswald's former landlady told my informant that one day, after her tenant and Marina Oswald had been quarreling, a "tall dark man in a white convertible" came to the house to pick up Mrs. Oswald and the baby. Oswald himself watched them as the baby's crib was carried to the car; he "just stood in the door, watching the group drive away. He didn't say anything." Marina Oswald was gone for "a week or ten days," according to this story, but eventually returned. The Oswalds stayed as tenants of Mrs. Tobias from November, 1962, until March 3, 1963. When he arrived, he was requested to fill out a card which asked him to declare his occupation. Oswald wrote a cryptic answer: "Service." This card was requested by the F.B.I., and Mrs. Tobias said it had not been returned. When Oswald left, he was entitled to a refund for the unused portion of his rent. Mrs. Tobias said he left without requesting it.

Oswald met Mrs. Ruth Paine, who was to become Marina Oswald's closest friend and her eventual landlady, at a party in late February, 1963. The story of their meeting is related by the novelist Jessamyn West in the July, 1964, edition of *Redbook*. Mrs. Paine said a friend invited her to his home to meet Oswald and his wife "because he knew I was interested in learning the Russian language well enough to teach it." Oswald expressed his dislike of the Soviet system, and he was particularly bitter at the fact that his mail had been censored. He said that, by good luck, "our embassy refused to surrender his passport to the Soviet government," otherwise he might have had to stay there.

Oswald and his wife, it is reported, also were frequenting Russian émigrés at this time—hardly a milieu where left-wing causes would have been supported. Yet a few weeks later Oswald suddenly became the leading Dallas champion of Castro. He wrote to the national Fair Play for Cuba office in Manhattan, telling how it happened. "I stood yesterday for the first time in my life, with a placard around my neck," said Oswald, "passing out fair play for Cuba pamphlets, etc. I only had 15 or so. In 40 minutes they were all gone. I was cursed as well as praised by some." He asked them to send him "40 or 50 more of the fine basic pamphlets," adding, "I do not like to ask for something for nothing but I am unemployed." They sent the pamphlets he requested.

Oswald lost his job in an engraving shop in Dallas shortly after he distributed his pamphlets. In late April, he announced that he was going to New Orleans. Mrs. Ruth Paine, who was now Marina Oswald's best friend, offered to drive Oswald's family to join him, when he found a job and an apartment. This was a 500-mile trip, each way. In September, after Oswald had lost his New Orleans job, Mrs. Paine came back and invited his wife to live with her, in her home near Dallas. She had, meanwhile, asked "a Quaker friend" to "look in on" the Oswalds during their stay in New Orleans.

The chief consequence of the New Orleans trip was to permit Lee Oswald to extend his operations on behalf of the pro-Castro forces. He set up a "chapter" of Fair Play for Cuba and proclaimed himself the "secretary," although no one at the national headquarters ever authorized this action. Some of Oswald's letters to the New York office of this group were strangely worded, for someone who was supposedly in sympathy with their objectives. He wrote once, for instance, that he had composed a circular which he admitted might seem "too provocative," but he said he felt that the important thing was "to attract attention, even if it's the attention of the lunatic fringe."

It did not take long for Oswald to "attract attention." On August 5th, he went into the store of Carlos Bringuier in New Orleans and began a conversation. Bringuier was a delegate of the Cuban Student Directorate, an anti-Castro Cuban group. According to Bringuier, "he told me that he had been in the Marine Corps and was willing to train Cubans to fight Castro. He also said that he was willing to go himself to fight Castro." He offered money to the anti-Castro cause, which Bringuier, who suspected he was an agent provocateur, says he refused. On August 9th, just four days later, Bringuier found Oswald on the street distributing pro-Castro leaflets. Oswald was in an embarrassing position. He could not admit in public that he was a double agent; and when Bringuier, backed by numerous supporters, tried to hit him, Oswald spread his arms and offered no resistance. "O.K., Carlos, if you want to hit me, hit me," he told his assailant. It will be observed that Oswald's gesture seems at total variance with the aggressive and pugnacious disposition which has been attributed to Oswald, who was neither pacifist nor coward.

That Oswald was a double agent in New Orleans is beyond discussion, and the only point remaining to be clarified is: Which side was Oswald betraying—the pro-Castro or the anti-Castro Cubans? An important clue may be the fact that next month, when he went to Mexico City, he checked into the Hotel Commercio. The Washington bureau chief of the Buffalo *News*, N. S. Finney, asserted on February 8th that this hotel is noted for the fact that it is "substantially used by Cuban exiles."

In a lecture series sponsored by Billy James Hargis, the extreme right-winger who heads the "Christian Crusade," Bringuier asserted in June, 1964, that when he and Lee Oswald were arrested and brought to the police station, there were two members of the F.B.I. there. Bringuier said these agents asked Oswald to identify pro-Castro sympathizers in New Orleans, and Bringuier declared Oswald replied, "I'll tell you, but not in front of Bringuier." The anti-Castro Cuban said that he was then requested to withdraw, and did so.

F.B.I. Director Hoover stated on March 7th: "To set the record straight, and to refute the misinformation which has been maliciously circulated, I want to state unequivocally that Lee Oswald and Jack Ruby were never F.B.I. informants; that they were never employed by this bureau in any capacity; nor did they render any services for or receive any money from the F.B.I."

This affirmation would deserve to be accorded greater weight were it not for the fact that Mr. Hoover and the agency he heads have, in the past, issued denials of this type whenever they considered it to be in the best interest of national security. In 1961, Congressman Morse, conducting an investigation of wiretapping, asked Deputy Attorney General Byron White to state how widely this was practiced by the F.B.I. The answer he received was: "The Federal Bureau of Investigation advises that it does not utilize the devices referred to in your letter." That same year, however, Assistant Attorney General Herbert J. Miller, Jr., told a Senate committee that on an average day the F.B.I. had 85 wiretapping instruments in operation.

The F.B.I. acknowledges its agents checked on Oswald, on occasion; it denies that Oswald was cooperating with them. It was thus with honest pleasure that Dallas Assistant District Attorney Bill Alexander, not known as an F.B.I. admirer, revealed to the press a short time after the assassination that among the papers found on Oswald by Dallas policemen was the name of James P. Hosty, Jr., of the Dallas bureau of the F.B.I.—and even more indicative that he was willing to cooperate with Hosty was the fact that he had kept Hosty's telephone numbers, both at home and at the office, as well as the license number of the agent's car.

One might cite, as substantiating proof of the relationship between the F.B.I. and Oswald, the fact that the F.B.I. was able to provide the President's Commission with details of Oswald's income for the seventeen months preceding the assassination—$3,665.89—and analyzed its sources, and the way he spent it. Information of this nature would have taken longer for an agency to reconstruct than the time at the F.B.I.'s disposal in preparing the report, unless a good deal of the information was already in their records.

There was one more item in the records of the F.B.I. about Lee Harvey Oswald. This one is a little more confusing. In March, 1963, Oswald is said to have acquired the rifle which was destined to become, according to official sources, the assassination weapon. It appears the F.B.I. knew that he had it, prior to the murder of the President, for it was only one day later that the F.B.I. announced the details of its purchase, after tracing it to a Chicago firm which had received an order for mail shipment to "A. Hidell." The letter had been written by Lee Oswald. European criminologists say this fact was revealed too quickly to have been disclosed by an analysis of his handwriting. Moreover, Harry Holmes, postal inspector for the Dallas area, has been quoted as acknowledging that there was a "mail cover" requested on Oswald's mail. Thus one assumes the F.B.I., in one way or another, was aware on March 20th that Oswald had now come into possession of a deadly weapon. It was certainly their duty to have known it. Yet, despite Lee Oswald's turbulent career, no one took Oswald's rifle from him—even though they now say that they have good reason to suppose that on April 10th he had already used it to attempt a murder.

Who was Oswald's target on the night of April 10th? According to the F.B.I. and to Marina Oswald, it was the most dedicated enemy of John Fitzgerald Kennedy in the United States—a citizen of Dallas named Edwin Anderson Walker. Mr. Walker was, until the Kennedy Administration, a major general commanding troops in Germany. He used that post to pass out literature among the men that he commanded—literature from the John Birch Society, which had a rather low opinion of the President of the United States. The President, of course, was Walker's commander in chief, a fact which did not in the least deter him from continuing his anti-Kennedy propaganda. The result of this was that the general soon found himself in a civilian uniform in Dallas, from which he occasionally ventures forth to help defend the country from the menace of the Negro schoolgirls in the state of Mississippi. Walker has a number of flags on his front lawn. He used to lower them to half-mast each time that he felt that the United States, under the Kennedy regime, was headed for damnation—an emotion that he felt quite often. When Dallas officially apologized to U. N. Ambassador Adlai Stevenson for the attack against him, Walker flew his flags upside down. A short time later, when the President of the United States was murdered and the country was in mourning, Walker raised his flags to full staff once again. "My flags are always flown full staff now," Walker told a U.P.I. reporter, according to a December 10th dispatch from Dallas.

Walker lives on fashionable Turtle Creek Boulevard. Behind his house there is an alley, and the F.B.I. informs us that Lee Harvey Oswald, a few weeks after he had received his 6.5 Carcano, came into this alley on the night of April 10th and tried to murder Walker. Thus, we have the picture of our mighty hunter—the same deadly marksman who, in the Marines, had fired 191 out of a possible 250—stalking his immobile prey, who was inside his house now, seated at a desk, illuminated by bright lights. The sniper crept toward his victim, raised his trusty weapon, resting it upon a picket fence to hold it steady, squeezed the trigger . . . and he missed the general completely! Walker stated later that the only thing that saved his life was that he turned his head just at that moment. For a marksman capable of firing three shots in six seconds at a speeding car, however, that should not have been completely disconcerting. Oswald benefited from complete protection. Why did he become so easily discouraged? One will never know the answer to these questions. We can only state that his intended target providentially was spared for new adventures.

Did Lee Oswald actually fire this shot? His widow says he did. But Walker's aides say that they know he didn't. And they ought to know. They brought in two detectives, formerly from Oklahoma City, to conduct their own investigation. They have checked the facts, and they say that they now know who tried to assassinate the general. It was "a former employee," according to the general's administrative aide, who told a source with whom I am in contact that the F.B.I. was given all this information, but persists in stating that the would-be murderer was Oswald. He said that the Birch Society was worried that this man might make a second effort to fire into Walker's window, and accordingly they take turns standing guard at night around his Turtle Creek home.

Certainly it does not look as though the weapon used had been a 6.5 Carcano. News reports after the Walker shooting say the bullet was a .30 caliber, and that it left a hole shaped like a golf ball. The Italian weapon handles smaller ammunition and is jacketed. There seems to be extremely little chance the weapons corresponded.

One of the discoveries of the police, after the Kennedy assassination, was a scrap of paper in Oswald's possession. It contained the one word "Walker," with the number of a telephone beside it. A reporter called this number, and it was, indeed, Edwin A. Walker's home. One must assume that Oswald's memory was very bad indeed if it was necessary for him to write down the name of someone whom he meant to murder. Did he have to telephone for an appointment?

When Marina Oswald testified before the President's Commission for the second time, she was asked if her husband ever had attended any "political meetings" shortly before the President's assassination. She had made no charge of this sort in her previous appearance, but this time, it is reported, she replied in the affirmative. Commission members were unable to obtain details about these meetings. But there is one public meeting which Lee Oswald did attend, which certainly could be called a "political" assembly. That took place on October 23rd, and the main speaker Oswald went to hear was . . . Edwin A. Walker, of the Birch Society. We shall return to this point later.

*   *   *

What Lee Oswald told the F.B.I. in the First District station of the New Orleans Police Department August 9th is likely to remain their secret. Twelve days later, though, he spoke in public. After the New Orleans papers had reported the arrest of Oswald as a Castro propagandist, he and his opponent, Bringuier, were invited to debate the Cuban question over the New Orleans radio station WDSU. The program took place August 21st. Oswald identified himself as an official of Fair Play for Cuba, which was totally without foundation, and proceeded with an exposition of the Castro theses which would certainly have shocked the New York office, starting with the statement, "Yes, I am a Marxist!" and continuing in terms well calculated to antagonize all possible supporters.

The inevitable happened. Oswald lost his job. Then, penniless—unless he had some source of funds not yet acknowledged—he set blithely forth upon his trip to Mexico; returned to Dallas, still without a job, and rented a small room under the name of O. H. Lee. The alias he used to his landlady at 1026 North Beckley Avenue cannot have been intended to protect him when he went job hunting. Oswald gave his right name in applying for the book depository job. The alias must, therefore, have had some connection with the other work Oswald was doing.

That this "other work" had anything to do with his Fair Play for Cuba activity would seem unlikely. In New Orleans, he had even tried to put crude posters in support of Castro on display outside the house where he was staying, "to attract attention," but his landlord took a dim view of that and compelled him to remove them. It would seem that Oswald's alias in Dallas was related to his role as double agent.

If Lee Oswald had been worried that he would not find a job in Dallas, it would not have been surprising. The job opportunities in Dallas for a man of Oswald's background scarcely could have been regarded as much brighter than they had been in New Orleans. His subversive reputation was, in fact, more of a liability in Dallas than in any other city that he could have chosen.

The police of Dallas knew him, not just from his previous reputation in New Orleans, but because they had already been in contact with him, when he passed his leaflets out in April. An anonymous informer telephoned Police Headquarters with a tip that Oswald was out on the street, distributing pro-Castro leaflets. The police checked on this story, spoke to Oswald and presumably required him to identify himself. They did not arrest him, but in any city as obsessed with Communist activity as Dallas, it seems hard to believe that they did not make a report about it. This would call for no mere superficial warning to Lee Oswald not to start a street disturbance; it would certainly provoke an inquiry on the suspicion that the Castro propagandist might adhere to the banned Communist Party—an offense which, as already has been noted, would have called for 20 years' imprisonment. Even if such proof had been lacking, any pro-Castro activity would, in the eyes of the authorities in Dallas, be considered proof that Oswald was a "sympathizer." It has been the policy of the "subversive squads" of many cities to advise employers of the Communist activities of any person that they hire. The F.B.I. is more discreet about it, but the threat of "exposing" people to employers, friends and neighbors certainly is constantly implicit; often it is the chief lever used by agents to persuade the person who is subjected to interrogation that he will lose his job if he does not cooperate.

A Communist in the United States today tends, therefore, to seek jobs which no one can take from him. Communists are independent taxi drivers, lawyers, dentists, farmers, or they borrow money to go into commerce, run small grocery stores or automatic laundries. Even self-employed persons thought to be "pro-Communist" are subject to the pressures which exposure of their sympathies entails. It is sufficient, for example, for the House Committee on Un-American Activities to go into a city and conduct a hearing in which witnesses are summoned to testify on Communist activities—even if those activities are of a purely propaganda nature—for the persons called as witnesses to be subjected to such pressures from the community that they are no longer able to earn a living, and are forced to move into another city. Doctors who are publicly identified as "Reds" lose half their clients; lawyers face disbarment; taxi drivers lose their permits; Communist shopkeepers are subjected to a boycott by their customers and their suppliers. Workers in a factory or office generally lose their jobs, and cannot find others.

All this would be true in any city. But in Dallas, Oswald's task was even harder when he went job hunting, and it is no wonder that, for the first week after his return from Mexico, he lived on unemployment relief. The mystery is that, only a few days after his checks stopped coming—he had, by that time, exhausted the benefits to which he was entitled—Oswald found a job in Dallas. And this job was not an ordinary one. The company he worked for was the one supplying textbooks for the schools of Dallas, through a contract with the state of Texas. A less likely spot for an acknowledged Leftist to retain his job, once the police had spoken to his boss, can scarcely be imagined.

Yet there was not just one "radical" in the school book depository on November 22nd. There were two. And they were both brought to Police Headquarters immediately after the assassination.

Mrs. Ruth Paine told Jessamyn West how Oswald got his job. "By the end of the first week he had no job, only his final unemployment check. The baby was due any day, and with no money and no prospect of any I think he felt pretty desperate. He got his job at the School Book Depository by chance. On Monday, October fourteenth, Marina and I were having coffee with a neighbor. We were saying that Lee had been unable to find work, and another neighbor who had stopped in said that she had a brother working at the Texas School Book Depository and that she thought there might be an opening there. When Lee called the house that evening we told him of this possibility. He applied and was accepted. Mr. Truly, the man who employed Lee, had two openings, one in a warehouse near Stemmons Expressway, one in the Depository building on Elm Street. Again chance entered, and Mr. Truly gave Lee the job at the Elm Street location." The neighbor to whom reference is made was Wesley Frazier's married sister, Mrs. Linnie Mae Randle, who was later to inform police that she had seen Lee Oswald carrying the package now presumed to be the Carcano rifle, as he entered her brother's car to drive to work at 7:10 A.M., November 22nd.

It has been argued that the reason Oswald kept his job at the school book depository was that neither the police of Dallas nor the F.B.I. had told his employer of his Leftist background. This exceedingly unlikely supposition is, in any case, an insufficient explanation. For there was already working at the book depository a bookkeeper who, accord-

173

ing to Police Chief Curry, was a "subversive." Curry said this man had been listed in the Dallas Police Department subversive files since 1955. And only a short time prior to the assassination, the municipally owned radio station of Dallas, WRR, is said to have mentioned him by name as an alleged Communist. According to a Dallas news reporter, the bookkeeper thereupon filed suit against the city of Dallas, and the suit was pending at the time of the assassination.

We have accordingly the totally unlikely supposition that, within one building, a book company wholly dependent on the state of Texas for its schoolbook orders would dare to retain upon its payroll not just one, but *two* notorious subversives, without some official sanction that would clear the company itself from being tainted with suspicion.

If police had notified the company and recommended that these men be fired, but the employer had refused to do so, it is certain that the Elm Street warehouse would have been one of the best-protected buildings on the President's parade route, for this conduct would have been regarded as exceedingly suspicious. In the absence of such action, one is forced inevitably to consider that, for reasons the police should now be able to provide, these men enjoyed some very high protection which was suddenly withdrawn the day of the assassination.

The bookkeeper previously mentioned "was never arrested, charged, or held in custody," Dallas police have told the President's Commission. They admitted, though, that they went to his home the night of the assassination, searched his home at 1:30 A.M. "with his permission," took him to Police Headquarters, where he was questioned for "6 or 7 hours."

There would seem good reason to suppose that if Lee Oswald had not been available to take the blame for the assassination, an effective substitute could probably have been provided.

*   *   *

Oswald got his book depository job October 14th, and he went to work the next day. One week later, he resumed the role he had been playing all his life: On three succeeding nights, Oswald was present at three meetings, of which the last two were organized by liberals, the first one by supporters of the Birch Society. The problem is, as always, to determine for which group Oswald was sincerely acting, and on which one he was spying.

In conformity with his consistent public image, Oswald said, of course, that it was only to observe the enemy in action that he went to the first rally, held October 23rd, at which the leading speaker was ex-General Edwin A. Walker, whom he is now charged with having tried to kill in April. Oswald made this statement at a meeting of the American Civil Liberties Union on October 25th, to which he had been invited by Michael Paine, a Bell Helicopter engineer who had once toured Europe as a singer. Paine was, at the time, in much the same marital position as Oswald himself; he was estranged from Mrs. Ruth Paine, Marina Oswald's landlady, but like Oswald he came once a week to see his wife. According to Jessamyn West, he and Oswald generally came the same night, and Mr. Paine says he tried, but without success, to alter Oswald's Leftist views. The Paines were reconciled a short time after the assassination.

Oswald told the Dallas chapter of the A.C.L.U. that he had attended Walker's meeting. He reported, with distaste, the general's alleged dislike of Catholics and Jews. The rally had been called in protest against the invitation that had been extended to U. N. Ambassador Adlai Stevenson October 24th, in celebration of U. N. Day. Right-wing forces had been organizing counterrallies. Walker, who regards the whole United Nations as a snare and a delusion, urged his backers to protest the rally scheduled to be held the next night at Dallas Memorial Auditorium. The picketing of Stevenson's address was organized by Walker's sympathizers, and the members of the Walker audience were urged to come again the next night and express their indignation.

Oswald came the next night, also. Washington *Post* reporter Ronnie Dugger wrote on December 9th "that when the Stevenson meeting of the night before was being discussed, Oswald nodded his head and said, 'I was there.' " This was the meeting in which Stevenson was shoved, struck, spat upon and cursed. *Newsweek* reported on December 8th, "When Ambassador Stevenson spoke in Dallas Memorial Auditorium, Oct. 24, pickets in the aisles chanted, 'Kennedy will get his reward in hell. Stevenson is going to die. His heart will stop, stop, stop and he will burn, burn, burn.' "

The vital question is, therefore, to learn on which side Oswald acted, on October 24th. This question has been answered in the Dugger article already cited. He quotes "a Dallas businesswoman" who did not want her name to be identified. This woman stated that she got to the auditorium early. There was a group of "well-dressed, neat youths" picketing with signs attacking Stevenson. Then a second group came into the lobby, also bearing anti-Stevenson signs. Oswald, she says, was among them. "These were a different type of people. Some were young, some were old. There were five to seven of them, and they were seedy-looking. He was clean, but he was very shabbily dressed. I remember thinking how pathetic he was." Is there any

176

possibility that Oswald was part of the pro-Stevenson audience, rather than his adversaries? Not according to this witness. She told Dugger, "I didn't see him anywhere else but in the lobby. He was picketing."

With this testimony, I will close the case against Lee Harvey Oswald.

*　　　*　　　*

Shortly after the assassination, former General Edwin A. Walker, in an interview with the right-wing German paper *Deutschen National und Soldaten Zeitung,* stated, "The death of Kennedy is by no means as astonishing as people now wish to make us believe. Too much explosive had accumulated."

Let us take a look at the "explosive" elements in Dallas.

It must first be stated that, contrary to the impression of some Europeans, it is not a city run by gangsters. *Fortune,* the most reputable spokesman of American financial circles, called Dallas in 1961 "one of the cleanest, best-managed cities in the country," meaning it was relatively free from criminal activity. The Dallas underworld does not give orders to policemen; they are used by the police and, just as long as they do not step out of line, they are permitted to take bets on horses, transport whores from one house to another and, in general, amuse the citizens and cater to their vices—to provide, in short, what in the Roman days was called a circus. U. S. crime is an extremely profitable circus, to be sure—with annual gross profits of 22 billion dollars, according to the F.B.I. director. Its promoters fight wars to the death with one another, but they do not generally fight with the police, who are their silent partners. In this sense of *silence,* Dallas can be said to be a model city.

The police do not run Dallas, either. Neither does District Attorney Wade, and neither does the Mayor, who told news reporters with a plaintive air that someone threatened to assassinate him also, if he went to Washington to take part in the President's funeral service. Nor is Dallas run by the people who inhabit it, by any person publicly elected, or appointed by officials chosen by the people. According to the *U.S. News & World Report* of February 3, 1964, it is run by the Dallas Citizens Council, "a group of top-bracket men, formed in 1936, who are willing to work to improve the city. Membership is by invitation only." The magazine says, "A visitor is told again and again" that this is "the group that really runs Dallas." A "veteran newspaper editor" is quoted as saying, "The Citizens Council, which actually runs Dallas, is a benevolent oligarchy. The council calls the shots on who will be placed on the ballot in elections for city offices. It's responsible for our record of clean government. We've never had a major graft scandal. There's no organized crime. There's some vice, of course, but there's no vice lord." And a "leading businessman" revealed, "The council is made up of men—about 250 in number—who are chief executive officers of important companies. They are men who have the authority to say 'yes' or 'no' in their companies. They have the habit of making decisions—and making their decisions stick."

A Dallas judge's daughter, in a recent book, describes these leaders as "The Decision Makers." All the members of the Citizens Council, she says, are businessmen, but above the Citizens Council there is a smaller group of the supreme elite—seven men of enormous wealth and power, who accept or veto any project of significant importance that is contemplated for this city of almost a million people. These seven men are too important to deal with the bureaucrats directly; they transmit their orders through the Citizens Council.

Control of civic matters is, in consequence, in the same hands which shape the business and economic life of Dallas. This is not unusual in itself, although I think that the degree of concentration of this power is exceptional in Dallas. What gives Dallas its chief character, however, is the nature of the industries on which it is dependent. There are two chief sources of the Dallas fortunes. One of them, of course, is oil; the second may be called, in its composite, the "defense plants."

In 1947 Robert W. Calvert, who was then the chairman of the Texas Democratic State Executive Committee, made the statement: "It may not be a wholesome thing to say, but the oil industry today is in complete control of the State Government and State politics."

What is the nature of the industry that runs the state of Texas? Oil itself is an intrinsic gamble, as the spokesmen for that industry keep saying, and they feel that since the risks are so great, no one would be willing to provide the money needed to locate and to develop oil wells unless there were compensating possibilities of more than ordinary profit. Even when geologists find reasons to suspect there is an oil deposit, only one well out of eight, in land where oil is not already being pumped from an adjacent well, turns out to yield oil in sufficient quantity to be commercially exploited. So the money spent on lease or purchase of the land, on research, labor and equipment is completely wasted, and must be deducted from the profits of the wells that do produce a fortune. This makes oil indeed a fearful gamble for the little man who has money for only one well or two. And even if an oil well is successful, even if it yields a profit which offsets the unsuccessful operations, oilmen say that they are in a different position from the manufacturer who builds a factory and goes into production. For a factory will last a long time before it must be replaced, whereas an oil well soon runs dry, and it is necessary to keep finding others. Oil producers feel, therefore, that they should get a tax deduction which permits them to subtract their hidden losses from their profits—losses due to the depreciation of their capital resources.

Congress has agreed that this is reasonable, and since 1926 a special supplementary deduction has been granted to the oilmen when they pay their taxes. In addition to the standard tax deductions to which other people are entitled, they receive a 27½ percent "depletion allowance" which they can retain from their gross income. Back in 1926, when taxes were extremely low, the oil industry's benefit from this advantage was comparatively modest, but today the most important factor in the plans of any wealthy individual or corporation is the way in which each operation will affect "tax status." Dummy corporations are set up and operated at a loss, for the exclusive purpose of permitting tax deductions by the corporation that controls them. Individuals establish charitable institutions and donate huge sums of money to them, while retaining full control of how these institutions manage their investments, so that they can claim a tax deduction which is practically equal to the money they donated and, by the manipulation of investments which they still control, increase the profits they derive from their own private operations. All these complicated calculations and maneuvers are designed to save an extra 5 or 10 percent of the gross income which the government would otherwise take from them—yet the Texas oilmen, who of course use these tricks also, have an enormous bonus, 27½ percent, from which the others do not benefit. The magnitude of this advantage can be judged from a comparison of taxes in the period when Congress voted this concession and their current level: for the five-year period from 1926 to 1930, the average annual tax collections of the U. S. Bureau of Internal Revenue were $2,895,868,000. By 1950, they had risen to $39,448,607,000;

in 1955, they were $66,288,692,000; and since that year, they have been mounting rapidly toward $100,000,000,-000. Thus, the income saved by Texas millionaires by this "depletion allowance" is now 30 times what it was back in 1926 when the concession was granted.

This huge concession is, however, only the beginning. It will be recalled that it was justified by the oil industry upon the ground that oilmen take more risks than other businessmen, and so cannot be as assured of making any profit at all. But they have simultaneously demanded, and were given, other tax concessions to reduce these risks until—for the big operators who have capital enough to take advantage of the riskproof tax provisions—any chance of losing money in sustained oil operations has been almost totally eliminated. If a company engaged in many simultaneous oil ventures digs a hole and finds no oil, the whole expense of this unlucky venture is deducted from the company's gross income. Even if the operation is successful, the producers are allowed, before they pay their taxes, to deduct "intangible expenses," which include the cost of geological surveys and such a high proportion of the price paid for equipment and for labor that all but 40 percent of the total cost can be subtracted before taxes are computed on the balance. What this means is that the gamblers who are likely to be beaten are the little operators who have borrowed money for a single operation. They are working with the odds against them—since most of the more promising oil sites belong already to the big producers—and the chances are that all their work will earn them nothing. They will even owe the interest on all the money that they borrowed. But big oil investors could not find a way of losing, over a long period of time, if they tried. Once you have passed a certain limit in the scope of your transactions, you can just sit back and watch your millions earn new millions. This must be extremely boring for a man who loves to gamble.

But there is a new trend that is dominant in Texas since the end of World War II: expansion into other industries than oil. There are two causes of this trend, historical and technological. The process gathered its momentum during World War II, when major aircraft factories were built in Dallas and, with government assistance, other war production plants, constructed for the military service, remained there. They continued to be used in peacetime to supply the Air Force with its bomber planes and radar. In addition, when the war had ended, Texas as a whole and Dallas in particular made every effort to attract employers from the North to relocate there, offering these powerful incentives:

1. Low taxes. In addition to the fact that Texas has no personal income tax, the corporate tax rate is lower than in most states.

2. Cheap labor. The predominance of giant cattle farms like the King Ranch has forced a large number of the farmers to move to the cities. The farm workers harvesting the cotton, rice and other crops have to compete with "wetbacks," migratory Mexican day laborers who work for pitifully meager wages; this, in turn, tends to force down the wages of the city workers in the factories.

3. Anti-union legislation. State laws forbid compulsory membership in a union; some types of strike are forbidden entirely; and, where a strike is allowed, no more than two pickets are permitted in each area of 50 feet. A union official arrested on a picket line is prohibited by law from holding any union office after that.

4. Natural advantages. Access to the country's principal sources of oil, natural gas and sulphur with reduced transportation costs.

With these advantages to offer, Dallas managed to attract

new industries to move there, supplementing factories built during World War II, and even these new industries tend also to be oriented toward contracts from the various armed forces. The most important was the aircraft firm, Chance Vought, which made the biggest industrial relocation in U. S. history, moving its entire plant from Connecticut to Dallas—a transfer of 13,000 tons of equipment from that Northern state, as well as the 1,300 most important employees (all the others were simply left behind in Connecticut to add to the Northern unemployed). Another major Dallas firm is Continental Electronics Manufacturing Company, which recently built for the Navy a $40,000,-000 radio transmitter, said to be the world's most powerful, designed to communicate with Navy submarines anywhere in the world, even when lying on the bottom of the ocean. Texas Instruments, which has rapidly become one of the nation's principal electronics parts suppliers, also has a large share of defense contracts.

What are the elements in Dallas which might lead to trouble for the two great industries—oil and defense—on which the area's economy depends? Who are the enemies whose intervention would be so feared that their very presence in this city might produce a situation that would be "explosive"?

For the oilmen, the response is clear—it would be anyone who contemplated a reduction of their tax exemption. Frank Ikard, a Texas Congressman, once called such persons "bomb-throwing liberals." The Texas oilmen are inclined to feel that epithet is much too mild; for them, the men who want to lower the oil depletion allowance are nothing short of Communists, although two critics of the present level of "depletion allowances" have been the late Republican leader, Senator Robert Taft, and former President Harry Truman, neither noted for pro-Communist opinions. Taft said it was "to a large extent a gift—a special privilege, beyond what anyone else can get"; and Truman charged, "No loophole in the tax law is so inequitable." In 1957, Senator Douglas of Illinois introduced a bill to cut this benefit, insofar as it applied to large producers, to 15 percent. The Douglas bill was beaten by a vote of 56 to 30, but among the 30 "Communists" who supported Douglas was a certain John Fitzgerald Kennedy of Massachusetts. In the 1960 Democratic platform, written by the Kennedy supporters, was a pledge to "close the loopholes in the tax laws by which certain privileged groups legally escape their fair share of taxation." It said "among the more conspicuous loopholes are depletion allowances, which are inequitable."

The Speaker of the House, Sam Rayburn of Texas, the oil industry's staunchest supporter in Congress, did his best to reassure his fellow Texans that these words meant nothing. "I've never heard of the 27½ percent oil depletion allowance being considered a loophole," he said. "I trust that the oil people do not consider it to be. I do not and never have." And Lyndon Johnson, Rayburn's protégé, declared, "The platform pertains to loopholes, and I see none in oil." But Texas millionaires were not convinced. In Dallas, their money and their votes went solidly to Nixon, who had made it clear that he proposed no change in the depletion allowance. Kennedy, however, was elected. In his last tax message to the Congress before his death, the President had proposed a serious reduction in the oil depletion allowance. It is known that he had planned to ask Congress to abolish such major tax loopholes during his second term in office, if he were elected with a large enough majority to offset the inevitable defection of members of his party from the major oil-producing states.

Who, then, was the chief threat to the Dallas oilmen? It must be apparent that their greatest enemy, in their opinion, was the President himself.

For a large number of the Dallas millionaires, however,

oil has ceased to be the major interest which it remains for most of Texas. Typical of these, and most successful, are the Murchisons, John D. and Clinton W., Jr., who were in 1961 reported to have each amassed a private fortune of 150 million dollars, and who jointly owned or directed 100 companies with assets of more than a billion dollars. These two brothers are comparatively young men, and they realize the oil boom cannot last forever. Wells already have to be dug deeper than they used to, with a great increase in cost of the equipment and the labor. So they have embarked upon the most ambitious project Texans have thus far aspired to: *They propose to win control of the United States from Wall Street.* For the first time in the history of the United States, a serious competitor has now arisen which openly defies America's traditional financial center. If the Murchisons and others win their gamble—for they are essentially not businessmen but gamblers, like the Texas oilmen—the financial center of America will not be in Manhattan, or in California either; it will be in Dallas. Nothing less than that is their ambition.

War broke out between the Texans and New Yorkers in 1960, when the Murchisons were accused of using their positions on the board of Investors Diversified Services to gain special concessions on loans from that huge corporation to the companies they controlled entirely. I.D.S. is the largest mutual investment fund corporation in the world; it has $4,200,000,000 assets. The Murchisons were furious and yearned for vengeance, even though the charges were withdrawn against them. They decided to get control of I.D.S. themselves and, since not even they had the resources to buy up a controlling interest of I.D.S. directly, they decided to attack the holding company which controls 47 percent of the I.D.S. stock—Alleghany Corporation. Quietly, they bought up shares in Alleghany and, before New Yorkers noticed what the Texans were doing, they controlled almost the same amount of voting stock as the Manhattan operator, Allan P. Kirby. There ensued a desperate campaign by both sides to persuade shareholders who were neutral to help the competing factions. The Murchisons hired Bankers Trust Company to keep a day-by-day analysis of their position with each stockholder on I.B.M. machines and, by a careful study of the distribution of the undecided holders, they succeeded in obtaining the required proportion of the proxies—whereupon the elderly New Yorker who had previously controlled the Alleghany Corporation was removed from office and replaced by the triumphant John D. Murchison. It was such a startling and decisive victory for Texas that the Wall Street forces hurriedly united and soon counterattacked. The Murchisons attempted to use their control of Alleghany Corporation to transfer the full control of I.D.S. to their own interests—an operation which, when added to their previous resources, would have given them a five-billion-dollar empire. But the ex-president of Alleghany Corporation contended such a transfer was illegal, and his lawyers managed to uphold their point in court. The Murchisons then had no further wish to keep their Alleghany holdings and sold out, taking an 18-million-dollar loss on the transaction. Kirby, the seventy-one-year-old New Yorker, was then reinstalled in his old office. He had gambled most of his own fortune on the outcome, something the two Murchisons had not thought he would dare to do. "It was a matter of pride," Kirby explained. And so the Texas interests retired, angry and bitter to have lost this first important battle with their Wall Street adversaries, but determined that it would not be the last one.

Who is the main adversary, in the eyes of the ambitious men who run that portion of the industry of Dallas which is not directly linked with oil? It is not a person, but a section of the country, that same section which was so dra-

186

matically under fire at the last Republican convention—the Northeast, from its economic capital, New York, to its political capital, Washington. Both the economic and the governmental forces that they hated were, accordingly, embodied in one man in November, 1963—the President who had announced his plans to come to see them. He was a damyankee.

But there was one factor which, in my opinion, was still more explosive than the oilmen's fear of losing their exemption, or the regional ambitions of the other Dallas leaders. It combined these drives and gave them an emotional expression.

I believe the murder of the President was provoked, primarily, by fear of the domestic and international consequences of the Moscow pact: the danger of disarmament which would disrupt the industries on which the plotters depended and of an international *détente* which would, in their view, have threatened the eventual nationalization of their oil investments overseas.

The Arms Control and Disarmament Agency, appointed by the President in 1962, attempted to combat such fears, declaring, "Disarmament affords an unmatched opportunity for satisfying our most pressing needs," but emphasized that this was just the long-term goal; the short-range impact might well prove disastrous. *Newsweek*, reviewing the agency's findings February 19, 1962, commented: "At first glance, the problems are staggering. Defense work accounts for nearly 10 percent of the nation's output, and employs nearly 10 percent of the labor force; what's more, the work is concentrated heavily in some industries and geographical areas." As we have seen, this applies particularly to Texas. "In addition," *Newsweek* continued, "the defense program supports half of the country's research and development work. Without it, technological progress would slow to a crawl. Even the stock market, with its huge influence on the economy, would probably react sharply to the prospect of lower defense earnings. The panel concluded that, without firm action to ease the impact, a $5 billion yearly cut in defense spending could shrink the economy by $10 billion to $12 billion a year." If Kennedy succeeded in attaining real disarmament, however, in his second term, the United States was faced with a reduction not of 5 billion but eventually of 50 billion dollars.

The Dallas oligarchy shared with all right-wing groups in America a deep hostility to measures undertaken by the Kennedy Administration, in the months before the President's assassination, to improve relations with the Soviet bloc. The majority opinion in the U.S.A. has been that efforts by the President to find a basis for negotiations with the Russians ought to be encouraged. When we use the word "negotiations," we imply a willingness to yield on some points, in return for similar concessions. Otherwise, we are not asking our opponents to negotiate; we are demanding unconditional surrender and must be, accordingly, prepared for the eventuality that they will choose to fight. This is a gambler's choice; it is not a choice which would recommend itself to any cautious leader or to any responsible section of the business community. The Kennedy Administration in the U.S.A., Khrushchev in the U.S.S.R., and the most influential leaders in the two armed camps, conscious that any new world war, as Khrushchev said in 1962, "would be thermonuclear from the beginning," had come to an agreement, just before the President was murdered, to renounce the testing of atomic weapons. It was understood that this was just the first step to eventual disarmament.

There was immediate and vocal opposition to this treaty, and it came from the minority in both camps. The Chinese and the Albanians said that any treaty made with Wall Street would be worse than useless; it would mean the

Russians had placed peace above the independence movement of colonial peoples and the revolutionary movement of the workers. It would mean, in short, that they had made concessions—and the Chinese said that this was treason. Russians, answering these charges, held there were two factions in the U.S.A.: a peace group, represented by the President, which they felt would continue to be dominant; a war camp, headed by the Pentagon. The Chinese laughed at this distinction; they said all capitalists were the same— they differed only in their tactics, but their economic interests would impel them ultimately to engage in an imperialistic war. This war could probably not be avoided; it would be a grave blow to mankind, but it would not be fatal; it would mean the death of the old capitalist system. Khrushchev answered that the Chinese acted as if they were not aware of what a nuclear attack would mean; he said his nation and the U.S.A. would certainly destroy each other, and there would not be a victor.

In the U.S.A., the argument proceeded along similar lines, with the majority of businessmen, like other sections of the population, feeling that the Kennedy Administration should continue cautiously exploring possibilities of stabilizing the world situation. By an overwhelming margin, Congress ratified the Moscow pact. And yet there was extremely bitter opposition from such right-wing groups as the John Birch Society which, taking a position analagous to that of the Chinese, denied that there was any difference between the Communists of China and of Russia; they were all the same: the moment that they had the chance, they would attack us. These men proclaimed that a President of the United States who bothered to negotiate with the Communists was crazy; worse than that, he was a traitor. He was probably pro-Communist himself.

Of all sections of the country, none was more opposed than Dallas to all indications that an understanding might be reached between the President of the United States and Khrushchev; none was more convinced that the United States not only could survive a nuclear attack but could go on and win the war, especially if the United States had made the "first strike"—and that it might be worth it.

That, of course, would be a gambler's judgment—but the men who run the economic life of Dallas are, almost without exception, gamblers. Gamblers in the literal sense of that word, men who, as a gesture of bravado, bet $200,000 on a single ball game and who win or lose a million dollars in a night of cards. But gamblers, also, by the nature of the industries they manage, and the way in which they make their money—in financial speculation, or in digging oil wells where the odds are 8 to 1 against a well that is productive. Such work necessarily attracts men whose psychology is totally unlike that of their counterparts in steel or coal, in banking or insurance.

In the history of civilized mankind, societies have chosen kings to rule them; priests, dictators, businessmen and bankers. But in Dallas, we have one of the most powerful and wealthy oligarchies in the world, controlled—as no society has ever been before—by men whose instincts are not those of businessmen, but gamblers. I suggest the impact of this fact upon world history, in any country which possesses the atomic bomb, is terrifying.

If a man believes that, under certain circumstances, it is worth the risk of ending life upon this planet to achieve some national objective, he will hardly flinch at ending one life, if the chances are remote that he will be detected. It would only take one man of this type—just one Mr. X—one gambler, to conceive and organize a plot to kill the President of the United States, if he believed the odds were high enough that he could do it and escape unpunished. He would have to have a good lieutenant to make all the necessary contacts, someone who already held a job that would permit him to arrange the details. And, of course—and most essential—there would have to be someone on whom to throw the blame; someone, ideally, who would in fact be implicated, but who would be quietly disposed of before he could talk to the reporters, or to an attorney.

Until now, no man who killed the President of the United States has bothered to deny it. The acceptance of responsibility for an assassination is normally implicit in the crime. The act of murder is no more than half of an assassination. There remains the duty to explain the deed, to justify it to the public. Otherwise, it takes on the appearance of a useless crime, provoking only sympathy toward the victim.

There is one exception: When the crime will be attributed to forces hostile to the ones who planned it.

That financial backing could be found in Dallas for the President's assassination is a possibility which cannot be excluded. I am told by an investigator that in February, 1963, there was a meeting of "some very prominent Texas men" with a professional killer from Dallas to discuss "the possibility of doing away with Cheddi Jagan, Castro or both." A person present at this meeting stated, "We were going to have men go down to Mexico and pose as oil agents. When Castro came in, we'd get him." He named one prominent Dallas millionaire who "said we could have all the cash we needed."

There were also some armchair assassins, as attested by the television report of Dr. Albert E. Burke, former educational television consultant for the National Broadcasting Company, on Station KCOP in Glendale, California, after the assassination. Dr. Burke spoke of "the experience I had in the Dallas home of an American whose hate for this country's leaders, and the way our institutions worked, was the most vicious, venomous and dangerous I have known in my life. . . . It was a very special performance by a pillar of the American community, who influences things in his community. . . . He said things had reached the point where there seemed to be no way left to get those traitors out of our government except by shooting them out. . . . My host assured me—when I objected to his remarks—that he believed as he did because he was an anti-Communist."

*   *   *

General Walker was right. The climate of the city that he lived in *was* explosive on the day the President arrived there. One of those who helped to make it so was Bernard Weissman, who inserted the notorious black-bordered advertisement in the Dallas *Morning News,* the morning of November 22nd, which began with the words "Welcome, Mr. Kennedy" and then proceeded to insult the President with a long list of accusations, terminating, "Why have you scrapped the Monroe Doctrine in favor of the 'Spirit of Moscow'?" Bernard Weissman, Joachim Joesten notes in his book, served in Germany under the general and was converted by the Birch Society indoctrination he received there, under Walker's orders.

And Walker did his part, too. While the President was living, on the day he came to Dallas, Walker's flags were flying upside down. When Kennedy was dead, he changed them.

The President knew very well how bitterly his policies had been attacked in Dallas, but he chose to meet his enemies upon their own ground and reply to them, and in the speech which he intended to deliver in the city where he was assassinated, Kennedy had planned to make one of the most vigorous denunciations of their activities which he had ever uttered, accusing them of the mistaken belief "that peace is weakness." But he never got a chance to say those words, and those who hold the same views he did must now rise and say them for him.

Why did the President take such a risk? some people have been saying. For the torrent of abuse from Dallas was not limited to words alone. When Stevenson was there, it had begun to take the form of naked violence. Because of his own experience, Stevenson telephoned Kennedy aide Arthur Schlesinger, Jr., and urged that the President's trip to Dallas be canceled.

I believe the answer to the President's decision can be found in an event which had occurred a century before and which, as author of a book on courage as exemplified by lives of previous Americans, he certainly did not ignore.

It happened in a city which in 1861 had much the same hostility toward the President of the United States as Dallas had in 1963; a city in which I have spent most of my life, and where my ancestors have lived since they came to America three centuries ago from Scotland; a city where flags are still raised in celebration of Robert E. Lee's birthday.

Lincoln was elected President in 1860 and took office March 4, 1861. The President left Illinois on February 11th, planning a tour of Eastern cities on his way to Washington, where he would be inaugurated. The last city on this trip was to have been the only Southern city that he passed through: Baltimore. Alarming rumors had begun to come from Baltimore as he drew near it. Railroad detective Allan Pinkerton, posing as a Southern sympathizer, told of an Italian barber from Baltimore named Ferrandini who was in command of a secret military unit which planned to attack Washington if fighting started between the North and South; this man had announced to his men that he planned to kill the President, and they applauded. Asked by Pinkerton what measures could be taken to evade the police after the President's assassination, the would-be assassin said that this question had already been taken care of: "They are all with us. I have seen Colonel Kane, the Chief Marshal of Police, and he is all right." *

The plot is summarized this way by Carl Sandburg:

> The police chief at Baltimore was arranging to send only a small force to the railroad depot, where a gang of toughs would start a fight to draw off the policemen. Then the Ferrandini assassins would close around the President-elect and deliver the fatal shot or knife thrust.

Independent of the Pinkerton investigations were the ones conducted by the New York Superintendent of Police —whose name, strangely, was John A. Kennedy—who sent his own detectives down to Baltimore. So grave did they regard the danger that they went at once to Washington, reported it to a high army officer; the warning was transmitted to Lincoln by the Secretary of State, who sent his own son on the train to bring the message:

> A New York detective officer who has been on duty in Baltimore for three weeks past reports this morning that there is serious danger of violence to, and the assassination of, Mr. Lincoln in his passage through that city, should the time of that passage be known. He states that there are banded rowdies holding secret meetings, and that he has heard threats of mobbing and violence, and has himself heard men declare that if Mr. Lincoln was to be assassinated they would like to be the men. He states further that it is only within the past few days that he has considered there was any danger, but now he deems it imminent. He deems the danger one which the authorities and people in Baltimore cannot guard against. All risk might be easily avoided by a change in the travelling arrangements which would bring Mr. Lincoln and a portion of his party through Baltimore by a night train without previous notice.

* Carl Sandburg, *Abraham Lincoln: the War Years.*

This suggestion was reluctantly accepted by the President, but he soon regretted having listened to his counselors. His enemies immediately leaped upon it as an indication of "cowardice." "Lincoln ran from the first whisperings of danger," said the Louisville *Courier.* "The men who made the Declaration of Independence did not make it good in that way. They fought for their rights; Lincoln runs for his . . . and leaves his wife. They ought to swap clothes." And the Baltimore *Sun* said, "Had we any respect for Mr. Lincoln, official or personal, as a man, or as President-elect of the United States, his career and speeches on his way to the seat of government would have cruelly impaired it; but the final escapade by which he reached the capital would have utterly demolished it, and overwhelmed us with mortification." Yet in that same paper's news columns, the story is told of what happened when the train arrived the next day—the one that the Baltimore mob thought Lincoln was taking. "As soon as the train stopped, the crowd leaped upon the platforms, and mounted to the tops of the cars like so many monkeys until, like a hive of bees, they swarmed upon them—shouting, hallooing, and making all manner of noises." The President's son Bob was sighted, and was vulgarly insulted; an appeal had to be made to let Mrs. Lincoln and her family leave the train unmolested. "The family and suite then alighted and were hurried through the side gateway." People still thought Lincoln must be with them. "The throngs, attracted by cries of 'Here he is!', 'There he goes!' swayed hither and thither with a force perfectly irresistible, and persons were knocked from the platforms and trampled on, and others had their clothing torn, one man having his coat ripped from his back." Infuriated by their inability to express their hatred of the President in person, the Baltimore crowd of 10,000 directed the intended violence upon any of his supporters who were present. The Baltimore *Sun,* with evident approval, notes:

> After it became apparent to the multitude that the President-elect had indeed escaped their attentions, they turned about to bestow them upon such of his humbler constituents whom they recognized in their midst. These attentions were exhibited in a system of crowding and squeezing exceedingly unpleasant to those upon whom the "pressure" was brought to bear. . . . A number of young men, bent on fun and mischief, seized a colored man driving a horse and wagon through North Calvert Street, and several attempted to chalk "Abe Lincoln" on his back. . . .*

Despite this concrete evidence that Lincoln's advisers had been right in guarding him from such a riot, which would certainly have been much worse if he had actually been there, Southern sympathizers insisted it was all a joke. *The New York Times* had this to say, however:

> The list of the names of the conspirators presented a most astonishing array of persons high in southern confidence, and some whose fame is not confined to this country alone. *Statesmen laid the plan, bankers endorsed it, and adventurers were to carry it into effect.*

One perceives that some things have not altered very much in the United States during 100 years. The work of Pinkerton and Kennedy reveals what an efficient, honest, loyal police force determined to guard the life of a President can do, despite the plans of statesmen, bankers and adventurers.

None of these men was punished, for the Civil War broke out a few days after Lincoln was inaugurated, and there was no time for an investigation of what, some assured him, had perhaps been only an "imaginary" plot. Police Chief Kane, as had been expected, openly sided with

---

* Baltimore *Sun,* February 25, 1861.

the South, although Baltimore was behind the Union lines. He was arrested, but escaped and fled to the Confederate States. A few years after the Civil War, Baltimore was comfortably back in the same status as before the war; it had a new police chief who had spent the Civil War as a Confederate officer who led raiding parties behind the Union lines which burned down bridges and destroyed the house of the Governor of Maryland. His name was Harry Gilmor, and he happens to have been my mother's uncle. . . .

Kennedy, knowing how Lincoln had been ridiculed and charged with cowardice, came down to Dallas, a predominantly hostile city. He relied upon the Secret Service, on the F.B.I. and the police of Dallas to protect him. Kennedy had picked a passage from the Bible which he planned to read there. He could not have known the terrible appropriateness of it. For that passage, taken from the Book of Psalms, was this: "Except the Lord keep the city, the watchman waketh but in vain."

The Lord did not, that day, keep Dallas. The watchmen were not looking in the right direction. Some of them, perhaps, thought Oswald was their *own* man; they did not know how many interests he represented. Since the President's assassination, these agencies have desperately sought to hide their own guilt by saying that it was a crime that could not have been anticipated, since it was the action of a lonely madman. Even if he were—and this, by now, has certainly been demonstrated to be false—he was *their* lonely madman, since they all had contact with him. But the insult is compounded when these agencies suggest discreetly that the President himself was partially to blame for his assassination—that he had a choice between the measures of security they recommended and "political exposure," and he chose the latter. It would seem that, having failed to find the real conspirators, perhaps because they did not ask the proper questions during their investigation, the investigators have just one accomplice to suggest—the man, they say, who made it possible for Oswald to perform the murder, a man who, like Oswald, is unable now to answer his accusers. The "accomplice" that they offer is the President himself.

The President of the United States went down to Dallas, trusting these men to protect him. But they failed him. We, the people, are the only watchmen Kennedy will ever have, now. Let these watchmen, then, awaken.

THE report that has been issued by the President's Commission has been analyzed in detail, in preceding pages. It is now appropriate, I think, to summarize its speculations —for they are no more than that. The incidence of "probably" and "This is how it *could* have happened" is a very high one.

SPECULATION: "Two bullets *probably* caused all the wounds suffered by President Kennedy and Governor Connally. . . . One shot passed through the President's neck and then *most probably* passed through the Governor's body. . . . The alinement of the points of entry was *only indicative and not conclusive* that one bullet hit both men. . . . The evidence indicated that the President was not hit until at least frame 210 and that he was probably hit by frame 225."

FACT: Refer to Commission Exhibit 893 (frame 210). Observe location of the crosshairs, showing where the President was shot. Note that a shot that passed through Kennedy at the position indicated would have struck the Governor in the lower portion of his back or hip, after first penetrating the car seat on which the Governor was sitting. Now refer to Commission Exhibit 895 (frame 225). Note that the car has turned toward the right, and that a shot fired at the point shown at the intersection of the crosshairs, after passing through the President, not only would have hit the car seat but would then have hit the Governor at the extreme left lower portion of his body or, if he were turning at that time, would have missed the Governor completely. Thus at no time between these two points could a shot have passed through Kennedy and then, while falling at an angle the Commission estimates at more than 17 degrees, "traversed the Governor's chest at a downward angle . . . and exited below the right nipple," as reported in the section dealing with the wounds. The evidence shows that two bullets hit the President, and that a third one hit the Governor of Texas.

SPECULATION: "Eyewitness testimony . . . supports the conclusion that the first of the shots fired hit the President. . . . If the first shot did not miss, *there must be an explanation* for Governor Connally's recollection that he was not hit by it. There was, *conceivably,* a delayed reaction between the time the bullet struck him and the time he realized that he was hit. . . ."

FACT: The Commission has provided its own answer to this speculation. The remainder of the sentence I have cited totally invalidates the first part: "—a delayed reaction . . . despite the fact that the bullet struck a glancing blow to a rib and penetrated his wrist bone." Flesh wounds can, of course, remain unnoticed for a certain time; a bone wound would produce an instant shock. The evidence shows that the shot which hit the Governor of Texas took place after Kennedy was hit.

SPECULATION: "It was *entirely possible*" for one shot to have been fired between Kennedy's two wounds, although "the gunman would have been shooting at very near the minimum allowable time to have fired the three shots within 4.8 to 5.6 seconds."

FACT: "A minimum of 2.3 seconds must elapse between shots," the report has stated. It must be remembered that this minimum is based on the best possible performance of the greatest rifle expert in the world; an ordinary shot like Oswald would require much longer. One shot in the interval between the President's two wounds would have to have occurred "almost exactly midway in this period. . . .

On the other hand, a substantial majority of the witnesses stated that the shots were not evenly spaced." Two shots between the President's two wounds would mean the speed with which one man could fire these shots had been exceeded. Testimony of the Governor of Texas indicates that he heard shots before and after he was hit. His wife confirms this. Testimony of the witness injured by the wild shot indicates he also heard shots both before and after he was hit. He cannot have been struck by any fragment of the bullet that hit Connally, since it was found intact. The evidence shows there were four or more shots, two of which were fired between the ones by which the President was wounded.

SPECULATION: "Based on the known facts of the assassination, the Marine marksmanship experts, Major Anderson and Sergeant Zahm, concurred in the opinion that Oswald had the capability to fire three shots, with two hits, within 4.8 to 5.6 seconds. . . . On the basis of Oswald's training and the accuracy of the weapon as established by the tests, the Commission concluded that Oswald was capable of accomplishing the second hit even if there was an intervening shot which missed."

FACT: The report states that six "expert riflemen" attempted to repeat the feat of the assassin. It appears that they fired at a stationary target, not one that was moving; the report, however, is ambiguous on this point. "Three marksmen, *rated as master by the National Rifle Association,* each fired two series of three shots. In the first series the firers required time spans of 4.6, 6.75, and 8.25 seconds respectively. On the second series they required 5.15, 6.45, and 7 seconds." Subsequently, "three F.B.I. firearms experts tested the rifle in order to determine the speed with which it could be fired. The purpose of this experiment was not to test the rifle under conditions which prevailed at the time of the assassination but to determine the maximum speed at which it could be fired. The three F.B.I. experts each fired three shots from the weapon at 15 yards in 6, 7, and 9 seconds." The evidence shows that, of the 9 series cited, fired by some of the outstanding experts in the U.S.A., the maximum time that has been attributed to Oswald, even if there was only a single shot between the President's two wounds, was exceeded by these men in 7 cases; that these experts, at least half of whom were firing at a stationary target, took an average of 6.75 seconds to fire three shots, and would, accordingly, have needed three more seconds to have fired a fourth one.

SPECULATION: "Constable Deputy Sheriff Weitzman, who only saw the rifle at a glance and did not handle it, thought the weapon looked like a 7.65 Mauser bolt-action rifle. . . . After review of standard reference works and the markings on the rifle, it was identified by the F.B.I. as a 6.5 millimeter model 91/38 Mannlicher-Carcano rifle. . . . [District Attorney Henry Wade] repeated the error that the murder rifle had been a Mauser."

FACT: The Commission notes the murder weapon "is inscribed with various markings, including 'MADE ITALY,' 'CAL. 6.5,' " etc. No consultation of the "standard reference works" was required to exclude the possibility that it was (a) a Mauser, which is German-made, or (b) a caliber other than 6.5. The error which has been attributed to Weitzman, therefore, could have gone no further. It would necessarily have been corrected minutes later at the first inspection of the rifle. The report states, "The rifle was identified by Captain Fritz and Lieutenant Day, who were the first to actually handle it." The evidence shows that the statement of District Attorney Wade was made after this first inspection of the rifle by the chief of homicide, a man equipped by training to identify a weapon, and that the first weapon found in the school book depository was, in fact, a Mauser, as Wade stated.

SPECULATION: "Howard L. Brennan was an eyewitness to the shooting. . . . Brennan described the man to the police. This description *most probably* led to the radio alert sent to police cars at approximately 12:45 P.M. . . . It is *conceivable, even probable,* that Tippit stopped Oswald because of the description broadcast by the police radio. . . . Brennan *could have* seen enough of the body of a kneeling or squatting person to estimate his height."

FACT: Brennan was brought to Police Headquarters on the night of November 22nd. Since glimpsing the assassin in the sixth-floor window, Brennan had been looking at a television broadcast in which Oswald's picture had been shown, and Oswald had been named as the presumed assassin. Oswald was brought in, with other men, and Brennan was requested to select the man whom he had seen. He was unable to make any positive selection. It was not until December 17th, after an interview with F.B.I. men, that this witness said he now was certain Oswald was the man whom he had seen on the sixth floor. The evidence shows that a witness who could not identify a man himself—even when marked with bruises from his fight with the police—could not have provided information so precise as to permit another person to identify him from a short statistical description.

It may thus be shown that the report of the Commission is dependent on a series of hypotheses which range from "probable" to "possible" and ultimately to "conceivable," on points as vital as the sequence of the shots, the interval between them, their direction, from what rifle they were fired, the shooting skill of the assassin, and the way in which the murder suspect was identified when the police first ordered his arrest. If any of these guesses should be wrong—and one would be sufficient—the whole edifice would tum-

203

ble and the awful fact of a conspiracy would have to be acknowledged and eventually dealt with.

Have you any evidence of this conspiracy? I have been asked. I have. It is the evidence presented by the President's Commission. For to prove conspiracy in this assassination, it is not essential to find witnesses who saw two men fire rifles. It suffices to provide the proof that one man could not have accomplished the assassination without help. I base my case upon the volume titled *Report of the President's Commission on the Assassination of President John F. Kennedy.*

Could a shot fired from the sixth-floor window have passed through the President's neck and then struck the Governor high in the back? I offer as Exhibit One the photographs taken from this position, shown on pages 102 and 103 of the report.

Could the first shot have hit the Governor of Texas? I refer the reader to the statement of the Governor of Texas and of Mrs. Connally, which have been summarized on page 112 of the report.

Could a 6.5 Carcano rifle have been thought, for more than a few minutes after it was found, to be a 7.65 weapon of German manufacture? I submit in evidence Exhibit Two, a picture of the rifle with the words MADE ITALY upon it, on page 83 of the report.

Accumulation of this evidence, and other facts to which I have referred, is an important service the Commission's staff has rendered. It would be a serious mistake to underestimate the value of this data. There remains the task of its evaluation.

Facts, such as the ones in the report, are subject to the most diverse interpretation. This book and the findings of the President's Commission are each based upon essentially the same facts. Those who hasten to acclaim the speculations of the President's Commission as the final word of history upon the subject would do well to place their judgment in perspective. This is not the first time that we have been told, "The case is closed." That statement was made by District Attorney Henry Wade within the first few hours after Oswald had been murdered. Wade said there was no doubt that Oswald had been guilty; he declared he had the facts to prove it, and "had sent men to the electric chair" with evidence that had been less convincing. Here are some of the interpretations Wade gave to the evidence in his possession.

SPECULATION: Wade told newsmen, "The next we hear of him is on a bus where he . . . told the lady—all this was verified by statements—told the lady on the bus that the President had been shot. . . . The defendant said, 'Yes, he's been shot' and laughed very loud."

FACT: The President's Commission calls this "an error apparently caused by the bus driver having confused Oswald with another passenger who was on the bus after Oswald had left."

SPECULATION: The police stated and Wade repeated that a map found in Lee Oswald's room had the trajectory of the intended bullets traced upon it in advance, proving premeditation.

FACT: The President's Commission says the map was one that Oswald used while hunting jobs in Dallas.

SPECULATION: The police said they had evidence that proved that Oswald ate a chicken while he waited to commit the murder. They said that his fingerprints were on the bag that held the chicken.

FACT: The President's Commission says the chicken bones "had in fact been left by another employee who ate his lunch there at least 15 minutes before the assassination."

SPECULATION: Wade said Oswald first became a suspect when employees working in the book depository were assembled by their supervisor and a roll call taken at which one—and *only* one—of them was missing. He said this occurred within the first few minutes. "Every other employee was located," Wade asserted. "A description and name of him went out by police to look for him."

FACT: The Commission states, "The police never mentioned Oswald's name in their broadcast descriptions before his arrest. . . . His absence was not noticed until at least one-half hour later. . . . It was probably no earlier than 1:22 P.M., the time when the rifle was found." There had been no roll call until that time. Tippit, meanwhile, already had been murdered.

Data, then, is of no value when accorded false interpretation. The sheer weight of testimony taken by the F.B.I. and Secret Service * is no indication that the meaning given to it by investigators is the right one. Much of this huge mass of data is conflicting. Witnesses have contradicted one another. There are many people, for example, who believe they saw Jack Ruby with Lee Oswald, prior to the Kennedy assassination. Ruby swears it never happened. The Commission seems to feel that Ruby told the truth, and that the other witnesses must be mistaken. Reasonable men might disagree with this conclusion.

Reasonable men, indeed, might disagree with many of the findings of the President's Commission—and throughout the world most people do, in fact, reject them.

I do not believe this case is closed. I do not think it will be, until some more satisfying answer has been given to the question which aroused the world: Why was the President of the United States assassinated? I believe we do his memory no service in pretending no one but a lonely madman could have wished him dead. If this were so, his death would have no meaning. I believe he lived for something, and I think he died for something. Any man is measured

* The Commission did not have its own investigators. "Because of the diligence, cooperation and facilities of Federal investigative agencies, it was unnecessary," their report states.

by his enemies. The list of those who hated Kennedy the day he died does honor to him. It must never be forgotten that he went to Dallas to combat these men, to tell the people of that city, of the nation and the world beyond that peace was not a sign of weakness.

Neither is ability to face the truth a sign of weakness. It would be interpreted, throughout the world, as evidence of the maturity of the United States. For we are not dishonored as a nation by attempts to find the murderers among us, but by our attempts to hide them.

It is not the light that we must fear; it is the darkness.

DATE DUE

JAN 1 5 '85			
MAR 21 1991			
FEB 4 1992			
DEC. 1 6 1992			
MAR 1 5 1995			
GAYLORD			PRINTED IN U.S.A